GET **WRITI**]

How **Anyone** Can W

An Inspirational and Practical Guide
to achieving your dream of
writing a book!

By

IAN C.P. IRVINE

Copyright 2019 © IAN C.P. IRVINE

Copyright 2019 © The IRVINE METHOD

Dedicated to Douglas McKell, Sue Alexander, Al Guthrie

And to my Parents

who taught me how to spel.

Table of Contents

Chapter 1

Introduction

It's said that everyone has a book within them. I don't know who said that, but I've heard it said several times and I think it's probably true. Today, more than ever, people are deciding to look inside themselves to try to find that book, to 'extract it' and then give it to others.

Some people are doing it because they dream of making vast fortunes from their literary prowess, and are hoping to retire from their work and move to a Caribbean Island where they sip cocktails all day and spin out another best-selling thriller on their laptop in the shade of a coconut tree.

Others are doing it because it's on their bucket list, and having climbed Everest, or more likely swum with dolphins or jumped out of an airplane with a large piece of cloth attached to their back - and survived - then writing a best-seller is next on the list.

And why not? In theory, writing a book has never been easier. Thanks to the new and exciting worldwide 'Indie Publisher' movement, almost anyone can write a book and publish it. And perhaps even sell a few copies. Or a few million.

In the old days, and we're talking less than ten years ago here, if you wrote a book, either it had to be incredibly good, or you had to have a contact in the publishing world who was willing to take a chance on you. For most people, the fear of rejection put them off ever trying. In fact, rejection and publishing were, until quite recently, almost the same word. First you would get rejected by your friends, for writing about them, then you would get rejected from all the agents you wrote to. If you did find an agent, then your book would almost definitely be rejected by all the publishers to whom it was sent. Even if it wasn't, and it *was* published, if it didn't sell enough, your book was promptly dropped and you'd probably never be published again.

Today, however, that's all different. Anyone can write a book. Anyone can publish it. And anyone can buy it. Even better, if no one buys the book, nothing bad happens. But, and this is the best part, it's highly likely that if your book is any good whatsoever, you will sell anything from at least one to your mum, to perhaps hundreds, thousands or millions, depending upon a combination of luck, how enjoyable the book is, how good the front cover is, and how proficient you become at doing your own advertising.

Also, on the plus side, is the fact that there are now possibly hundreds of books out there that tell you how you can join this publishing revolution, and how you too can become a successful Indie Author. Most of these books tell you about the mechanics of how to use the technology that's out there to support you in your Indie Adventure. They explain how Amazon KDP works, for example, or how to run adverts for your books on Facebook or Instagram, or even Amazon itself.

Unfortunately, however, there are few books or courses which help you overcome that same problem which has dogged would-be authors for hundreds of years: how to 'extract' that first book out of you. And then the next. And possibly even a third.

You might have heard a rumour that writing should be fun. Most writers write because they feel they *have* to write. They feel *compelled* to write. So, if you want to write too, but fear the process of 'book extraction', how can we change your attitude, so the process no longer feels so daunting? How can we make book writing fun? How can we change your viewpoint and remove the trepidation and help you to really WANT to write, and look forward to it? How can you arrange it so that your writing flows easily, that there is little effort spent on *making* yourself write, and that all your effort is spent on the actual writing itself?

How can you *motivate* yourself to write so that it's the number one thing you want to do, and that *not* writing now becomes the *abnormal*? How can you transform your wish to write a book, into a compulsion that drives you to write during every possible moment where you can put pen to paper? In other words, how can you become – a 'writer'?

Hopefully that's one of the things you will learn here, today.

In this short but informative book my goal is to quickly share with you a new method which I have developed specifically for authors, which anyone can use to motivate themselves to write a book. For the sake of this book, let's call it the Irvine Method™. I'm not going to spend a lot of time teaching you things which you can read about in any of the other books you can already buy. Instead I'm going to try to teach you two or three key things that I had to learn for myself when I started out my writing career and which I don't think you can learn elsewhere.

Since then I've had almost two million books downloaded from Amazon, and have written twenty-two books, all thrillers, many which are considered not bad. (I'll leave it to you to check them out if you want, and to formulate your own opinion on whether they are any good or not – www.iancpirvine.com.)

In general, using the Irvine Method™ I'll share in this book, it takes me between two to six months to write a two-book series, and then about fifteen minutes to publish them on Amazon. During that time, I also have a full-time job and a family to bring up.

The main point here is, that I am MOTIVATED to write. I *want* to. I look forward to it. And in general, there is no need to 'extract' a book from my creative mind… it just flows. In the process I will share with you in this book, one of the first things I do before I start a book is to do a mental exercise which enlivens my brain and plants the seeds of motivation into my subconscious. Once this is done, my subconscious becomes hard-wired into producing the next book. And from there on in, I'm on autopilot until the words 'The End' appear on the blank page in front of me, and I realise I have just finished the first draft.

Don't worry, I won't abandon you there. As well as sharing with you how to set up the process of writing a book and motivating yourself to do it, I will also share with you some tips on the writing process. I'll follow this with some general guidance on how to edit it and get it into a place where it's ready to send to a publisher or self-publish.

The interesting thing about this process is that although I've applied it to writing a book, key parts of the process can also be applied to many other aspects of life. One of the tips I'll share with you is a good trick on how to overcome those sometimes seemingly impossible problems you may encounter in your daily life.

For the price of a cup of coffee, you really have nothing to lose, but everything to gain.

So, let's recap what this book will be about: it's not only about how to write a book, it also tries to answer the question of how to get that book out of you, onto paper/or into a Word document and then printed for others to read.

So how do you start?

The simple answer is you start at the beginning.

Chapter 2

Step1: A Good Title

In the Irvine Method, Step 1 and Step 2 can be interchangeable, and are flexible, depending on whether or not you already have an idea for the book. Let's assume just now that you don't have an idea.

That you literally have no idea what you are going to write about, only that you do want to write a novel.

This is the situation that I have often found myself in: I've just finished a book, and I want to write another one, but I don't know what it will be about. I just know that I want to start it as soon as possible!

When this is the case, the approach I adopt is to try to come up with a name for the book first, and then to write the book based around the name.

At first, this may sound crazy, but actually it's not.

It's all part of the Irvine Method, which, as you will discover as you read this book, is all about letting your imagination and your subconscious do the work for you.

With the Irvine Method, the basic idea is to first think of a good title. Something that catches your imagination, and will look good on a front cover. It has to be snappy, to the point and if possible, to immediately capture the interest of your future readers. (*'This book sounds good. I wonder what it will be about?'*).

Part of this step is to try to visualise for the first time, in a simple way, what the title will look like on a book cover. You don't have to go into too much detail at this stage in terms of cover design. Just basically, does the title sound good, and do you think it will fit easily into the confines of the small thumbnail that all books are now judged by on the product pages of Amazon?

A good exercise at this point is to sit down at your laptop and go to the Top 100 Paid books in your country and spend an hour just going through the charts, looking at what types of covers you can see. In particular, look at the titles of the books, and absorb any trends you see for that genre. Different charts have different types of covers and titles. For example, a Crime Thriller book cover and title, exudes criminality and mystery. A cookery book makes your mouth water.

When you begin to feel in your writer's bones the sort of snappy titles that are being created and published, then you can move on to the next step, which is to think of your own title.

Before doing that though, I just want to say something else about the other aspect of a good title, which is particularly important to the Irvine Method. This is to let the title act as a trigger to your subconscious which then sparks your mind into generating a story based around that title.

In other words, you choose a title that sounds interesting, and then you write the whole book based around that title!

This is how I have written half of my books, e.g.:

Haunted From Within
Haunted From Without
I Spy, I Saw Her Die
The Assassin's Gift
The Messiah Conspiracy

Taking *Haunted From Within*, for example, my wife and I were throwing around what we thought *could* be catchy titles, in different genres, and she suggested, "Haunted From Within".

I immediately latched on to the idea and decided that was it!

Personally, I thought it sounded really intriguing.

I thought the title sounded catchy, and that readers may be attracted to the book, based upon the title.

In my mind's eye, I could easily see how just those three words would fit on the thumbnail cover of a book appearing on Amazon.

So, I decided that I would write a book based on that name.

At this point I knew it was important to move on to the next step in the process and to decide what type of book it was going to be. Deciding this quickly, would then influence your subconscious and guide it to start formulating what the book would be about.

So, onto Chapter 3.

Chapter 3

Step 2: Having An Idea: What's The Book About?

Sometimes Step 2 comes before Step 1, but today let's just assume we've already come up with a title – we'll talk about the other way around shortly afterwards.

So, the big question is now, 'What's the book going to be about?'

In your mind's eye, is this book a thriller, or a romance? Or a book about flowers, or cooking? (i.e. Fiction or Non-Fiction)

At this point, perhaps you actually don't mind what type of book you're going to write, or in which genre. Or maybe you're already a crime thriller writer, or a romantic author, and you know the next book is going to be in that genre again.

In this case, you will invite the name of the book to conjure up ideas in your mind which are already guided by the genre you are interested in.

Alternatively, you may let the title guide you in a completely new direction.

For example, returning to the example of *Haunted From Within*, I was intrigued by the way the title suggested to me that a person was being haunted, but from within, and not from without.

How could that be possible?

That was interesting.

So, my mind started thinking about how that could possibly work.

However, I also wanted to write a crime thriller. It was just an inkling I had. Something that I wanted to try to do.

So now I had a small problem, potentially.

The word 'Haunted' suggested something paranormal. Something to do with ghosts.

I didn't particularly like that idea.

So, I didn't pursue it.

At this point I have an idea of a genre, and a title, but no plot.

The next step is to come up with an idea of what the book should be about.

How do you do this?

Before we move forward, I think we should take a side-step and consider something else.

The Irvine Method of writing a book relies heavily upon your subconscious doing the work for you. It consists of visualisation, listening to your thoughts, asking questions of your subconscious and believing that your subconscious mind will work out an answer and pop that answer back into your conscious mind.

For the Irvine Method to work, it will require you to believe in yourself and your own mind. So, before we move forward, I would like us all to consider a few examples which can demonstrate how powerful your subconscious mind is.

One of the points I want to illustrate here is that your subconscious mind is working ALL the time. Continuously thinking. Evaluating. Solving problems. Finding answers to challenges that you may set it. You may be totally unaware of all the work your mind is doing, but you can trust that it is doing it.

To illustrate this, I would like to suggest you do the following experiment. It may not work for everyone, but it should work for most of you.

And if it does work, you'll probably be amazed.

The trick I am going to teach you now comes from something I learned while travelling frequently with my work, and staying in lots of hotels in different time-zones.

The scenario is this: you're going to bed at night, and you know you have to get up at 7.00 a.m. in the morning. You set your alarm clock for 7.00 a.m.

For some of you reading this, you will perhaps already be familiar with the experience that just before the alarm goes off, you awake at 6.59 a.m., turn over and switch the alarm off just before it rings.

How does that happen?

If this hasn't happened to you, I would like to suggest you try the following: tonight when you go to bed, lie down on your back, tuck yourself in, make yourself comfortable, and switch off the light.

Now look upwards, into the darkness above your bed.

In your mind's eye, I want you to imagine a black rectangle with illuminated glowing red edges hovering above the bed just below the ceiling of your room.

Within the red-edged rectangle I want you to imagine in bright, glowing, red numbers, the time which you want to get up at.

6.58 a.m.

Imagine you can see the glowing letters.

Just like the display on a digital alarm clock normally found bedside your bed.

See the time you choose on the digital display above your bed, in your mind.

6.58 a.m.

Close your eyes, and 'set' that alarm.

Ask your subconscious to wake you at that time.

Now go to sleep.

It may sound impossible, but please do not be surprised, at all, when you awake the next morning at precisely that time you have imagined and requested yourself to awake at.

It's incredible.

But let's consider here what is actually happening.

Is your mind counting every second, and formulating every minute, and each hour, and counting down exactly until the moment you wish to awake - and then waking you up at exactly that time?

If not, how does it do it?

Meanwhile, while all this is happening, your conscious self is fast asleep!

This illustration, which, by the way, does work for many, many people, proves that while your conscious self is busy doing one task – like sleeping, or reading, or dancing, or driving, or watching TV, your subconscious mind can be busy performing a myriad of other tasks that you are completely unaware of.

Please, try the above.

You might be amazed.

Or perhaps you already know about the power of the human mind, and your own subconscious self?

'*But what does this have to do with writing a book?*' I hear you ask.

Actually, quite a lot.

Because now we know that on top of the many tasks it is already performing every second of every day, helping us to live and breathe and move and survive, we can also ask our subconscious self to add one more trivial task to its list: to help you come up with a plot for a book!

We're not yet looking for a detailed plot. Or a big plan.

All we want for now is a few simple lines which describe an overview of the story. It might be a formulated sentence, or just a feeling. An idea, or the germ of an idea.

A seed, which once you *trust* that this will happen, will grow and develop and become the book you've always dreamt of.

The way I suggest you do this is to go for a walk, or sit in your garden, or find somewhere you can relax for a couple of minutes. Somewhere you like being.

Somewhere you feel comfortable.

Breathe.

Relax.

Maybe even close your eyes – although this is not absolutely necessary.

Breathe deeply.

Relax some more.

Then think of your book. Imagine the title of the book written in your mind in bright colours.

Possibly even imagine the title written on a book cover.

Now *ASK* yourself the question, "*What's it about?*"

Ask yourself, "*How does it begin?*"

Ask yourself, "*How does it end?*"

Ask yourself, "*Who is the main character?*"

If at this point you still haven't decided what genre the book will be, then …

Ask yourself, "*What type of book is it? What genre? Crime? Romance? Science Fiction? Mystery? Suspense? A thriller?*"

Perhaps now close your eyes again, if you've opened them.

Think of the questions once more.

Then relax.

Take several deep breaths.

Open your eyes slowly.

And now get on with the rest of your day.

Over the coming days and weeks, ideas will begin to bubble up from your subconscious.

A genre will surface in your mind.

A basic idea.

Perhaps a few.

One of these ideas - which will suddenly, at some point, probably when you least expect it to, just 'pop' into your mind - will be one that immediately makes you latch on to it, and think, '*Yes, that's it!*'.

As I said, it might not be much. Just a phrase. A starting point. A seed.

But as soon as you nod to yourself and think, 'yep, that's the one', that simple idea will start to grow and develop.

Another phrase will pop into your mind.

An idea for a character.

A location.

A description of what will happen in the book at a very high level. Not a plan, just a feeling...

Never force it.

Just entertain it.

And ask more questions.

"Okay, I like the name Jack for the main character. How old is he?"

"What's his job?"

"Okay, I like the idea that this book is about a bank robbery/ a spy story/ a holiday romance... So, what do they steal?/ what do they spy on?/ who falls in love with who and where?

Ask questions. And more questions.

Develop the idea over time.

But don't wait until you have the whole plot before you start.

Start writing as soon as you can, and the rest of it will come to you...

But more on that later.

Don't be surprised, however, if a complete, detailed plot just 'appears' in your mind, almost all at once.

This can and will happen to some of you.

Did you know that some of the greatest composers heard *complete*, *new*, symphonies play in their mind, and struggled to write them down as fast as they could before they forgot them?

One moment their minds were blank, and then a moment later, they couldn't contain the complete, formulated ideas which they had.

Some people call this inspiration.

Others call it a miracle.

Perhaps, however, it is just you - your *subconscious* - working hard in the background, and then providing you with the answers to the questions you have asked of it!

In summary, the output from Step 2, is a quick, simple way to describe what the book will be about. (Not too complicated, maybe even just a one liner, but a description which captures what type of book it will be: a thriller, a murder mystery, a romance? It's your 'internal pitch' to guide you through the next steps of the process.

For example, in the case of *'Haunted From Within'*, my idea was:

'I'll write a crime thriller. It'll be about a man who see visions of murders taking place. The man's a reporter. He investigates the visions, and finds the murderer.'

After I had accepted this idea, the seed sprouted. I started asking more questions, and more answers and ideas popped into my mind.

Very soon the idea had changed to:

'I'll write a crime thriller. It'll be about a man who almost dies, but receives a transplant which saves his life. He then starts seeing visions of murders taking place. The man's a reporter. He investigates the visions, and finds the murderer.'

Very quickly this developed to:

"I'll write a crime thriller. It'll be about a man who almost dies, but receives a transplant which saves his life. He then starts

seeing visions of murders taking place. The man's a reporter. The reporter realises that the visions he is experiencing are the actual murders of the victims, as they take place, as seen through the eyes of the serial killer, whose organs are now inside his own body. He investigates the visions. The reporter realises that he has to discover the identities of all the victims, and then also identify the serial killer."

Then, focussing on the main character of the story a bit more, I got this:

"I'll write a crime thriller. It'll be about a man who almost dies, but receives a transplant which saves his life. He then starts seeing visions of murders taking place. The man's a reporter for the 'Evening News' in Edinburgh, Scotland. He's about thirty years old. His name is Peter Nicolson. He has a girlfriend but is not yet married. He is scared of heights. The reporter realises that the visions he is experiencing are the actual murders of the victims, as they take place, as seen through the eyes of the serial killer, whose organs are now inside his own body. He investigates the visions. The reporter realises that he has to discover the identities of all the victims, and then also identify the serial killer.."

All this happened in rapid succession. Possibly minutes.
From that, it was possible to sit down and move to the next stage.

Before we move on to the next chapter, we should consider for a moment, what happens to those of you who start with an idea for a plot, but don't have a title?

Actually, I think this is the easiest path of the two.

If you already have an idea, and you know what genre it is, then you are already half way there!

To come up with a title, we follow a similar process to above. You find somewhere you like, sit down, take a moment to yourself, and relax.

Ask yourself, "*What shall I call this book?*"

Now, as above in the other scenario, just get on with your life.

Very soon, a little idea will knock on the door of your conscious mind.

Don't be surprised if you love the title your subconscious gives you.

If you don't like it, close your eyes, shake your head, forget it, and then ... 'get on with the rest of your day'.

You know what comes next.

Very soon, a little idea will knock on the door within your mind.

And when it does, and if you like it, you're ready to read the next chapter.

Chapter 4

Book Length

In the Irvine process for writing a book, the author lets his or her subconscious mind do most of the hard work.

However, whereas the subconscious mind does the work, it's very much the case that the conscious mind must be in charge and provide the guidance.

The conscious mind has to ask the right questions at the appropriate times.

The conscious mind has to give praise to the subconscious mind when it creates a good idea or helps the author to write something very good.

AND… the conscious mind has to keep the subconscious mind under control, providing guidance about how long the book is going to be, and keeping track of progress throughout the book, speeding the action up when necessary, slowing it down at other times, and keeping the size, length and number of chapters under control.

Let me give you an example of why this is necessary.

Many years ago, I decided to write my first book. I never gave any thought as to how long it should be. I just knew I wanted to write a novel, and that I had a good idea.

So, night after night, I sat down, and wrote.

And wrote.

And wrote.

Eventually I saw two words appear on the page, which read "The End", and I realised that I had just finished my first book!

I was very happy.

When I did a word-count I found out that it was almost 300,000 words long.

It had taken me two-years.

I was very proud.

I had written my first book.

It was a few weeks before I discovered that no one would publish such a large book.

In paperback form it would be too large and too heavy. Distribution and freight costs would be very high. Printing costs enormous. The price of the novel would never recoup the costs.

AND, if despite all the odds, it was ever published, it would be prohibitively expensive to translate it.

Plus, this was my first novel. No one would take such a risk on an unknown writer.

I was very proud of my novel, but by now, I was a little concerned.

In fact, I was beginning to feel rather stupid.

This was in the days before ebooks.

However, even nowadays, I have discovered to my ongoing cost that many publishers are today looking for novels of around 100,000 words only.

Sadly, to this day, I continue to write large books, but now am often forced to split them into a series to make sense of what I have created.

The lesson from this story, is that even though you may become motivated to write, someone still has to keep hold of the reins and make sure you don't overdo it.

When I now look back upon my 300,000 word 'masterpiece'/disaster, I realise that I was very naïve. Rather stupid. And that I wasted many, many nights at my desk when I could have been out in the sunshine. Or writing another book, which, with better forethought could actually have been read by someone instead of gathering dust in the top drawer of my desk. My very own 'top-drawer' novel.

Where it still is to this day.

The lesson to be learned from this chapter is that before you start to write, you should set yourself a target length for your novel which is acceptable to both yourself and your customers and your audience.

If you are hoping to find a traditional publisher for the book, make sure you don't write too much.

If you want one of the many new ebook publishers to accept up your novel, then try to get a view from Amazon just how long the other successful books being published actually are.

I would suggest that you target about 100,000 words for both.

Before we move to the next chapter, I feel that I should also add that if you want to write a book, and it's not going to be a novel, you have lots of options open to you nowadays.

In particular, for people living in the UK, I just want to highlight 'Kindle Singles'. These are short books between five thousand and thirty thousand words. To learn more, go to your browser and type in 'How to submit Kindle Singles'. If you don't have the time to write a full-length book, this is perhaps another option you could explore!

Now, on to the next chapter…

Chapter 5

Plotter Or Pantser? How To Write The Book (Part One)

We're making progress.

We have a title, a genre, an outline of what your book will be about, and a target for how long the book will be.

The next step is to actually sit down and start to write the book.

To put pen to paper, or more realistically, start pounding the keyboard and make words appear electronically in a Word document.

At this point, some people will begin to feel uncomfortable.

"But I don't have a full plan yet?", you may hear them cry out in anguish and alarm.

Or,

"My wall is not yet covered in little yellow sticky notes? I haven't detailed all my characters? I don't even know who my characters are yet? How can I start? No... no... I'm not ready!"

To which I say, "Relax! You are ready! *Almost...*"

In a future chapter we will talk about 'The Beginning, the End, and the Middle' of your book. I'll leave that till then, but for now I would just say that starting a book without a clear idea of everything that is going to happen is fine.

It's okay!

In fact, it may even be preferable.

I know that some people want to have almost every minute detail worked out and written down in notes stuck all over their walls, or in overflowing notebooks, or detailed notes on their laptops which outline what each chapter will be about, but that's not completely necessary. It works well for some people, but for others it's just an excuse not to write the actual book.

I've heard of people, even met people, who spend years and years planning a book, but never actually start it.

If you're one of those people, then this book is *especially* for you.

The message of the Irvine Method, is that instead of doing all the planning *consciously*, and producing reams of detailed descriptions and plans, it's best to leave it to your *subconscious* to do this for you.

I've heard the expression 'Plotter' or 'Pantser' used before to describe those who plot, and those who just sit down and write, and seemingly fly by the seat of their pants.

At first, I thought I was a Pantser.

Now however, I realise that I am actually also a Plotter.

But, I let my subconscious do all the plotting. I trust that my subconscious brain is immensely more capable than my conscious self.

And from experience I have been amazed by the results it can produce.

In *Haunted From Within*, I started with one character, and the plot outline we discovered in the last chapter.

As I wrote the book, sitting down eagerly each day to type whatever came into my mind, new characters appeared without bidding, and starting walking across my pages and announcing themselves to the world, without even discussing it with me first.

Before I knew it, numerous sub-plots had emerged, all seemingly diverging in different directions.

I found it amazing.

It made me even more motivated to write, and to turn up at my keyboard each day just to discover what happened next!

What was supposed to be a difficult job of writing a book, became a joy and pure entertainment as I read about the characters in the story and discovered what they were up to. It was like reading a brand-new book, only that the words were appearing on the pages only microseconds before I read them.

Towards the end of the book, although I did begin to get nervous about how at least six subplots could possibly all come together before or in the final chapter, I trusted my subconscious and continued writing.

Incredibly, in the last pages of the book, they all did.

Unbelievably I hadn't consciously planned any of it, *not really*, because I was paying due respect to the guidance in Chapter 8 of this book - which was why I was nervous – but the truth of the matter was, that my subconscious had planned it all.

When I had finished the book, I read it again. And again.

And I was amazed to find that almost all of the loose ends that had emerged during the writing had tied themselves off before the final words 'The End' appeared.

Also, facts and figures which I have used or included or written about earlier in the book, then checked out and backed up future plotlines that emerged later in the book. All without conscious planning.

All amazing... as far as I was concerned.

But perhaps, all to be expected, if you trust your subconscious and understand the truly amazing power it has.

I think that what I have written in this chapter is really worth emphasising.

The most important part about writing a book, is starting.

The next most important part is - continuing.

Words appear. Characters come to say hello.

Things happen.

Interesting things. Surprising things.

Unplanned things.

In another of my books, 'The Messiah Conspiracy' the main character of the book was shot and killed one evening as I wrote a chapter.

I was shocked.

It was completely unexpected.

What should I do now?

The book was about the experiences of that character. He was the hero.

But now he was dead, with a bullet hole through this head...

Gulp!

By this time, I had written hundreds of pages... was it all a mistake? Had I wasted months of my life?

I took the rest of the day off.

Went for a walk.

A swim.

Had a beer.

Got even more nervous.

Yet, the next day I came back to my keyboard, sat down, and started to write again.

It turned out that another character soon evolved, took over the main role, and the book carried on.

In the end, looking back, the main character's death was not such a bad thing after all.

In fact, it was brilliant.

Completely refreshing.

I would like to claim no responsibility for that development in the story, but I suppose I should, because it was *my* subconscious that wrote that part of the book and which suddenly changed the direction of the plot, but then brought it all back on track later, to a successful conclusion.

I will today perhaps admit that maybe 'The Messiah Conspiracy' is not my best book, but I should say in its defence that it was my first commercial novel. The one I wrote after the '*300,000 word Top-Drawer Novel*' which I mentioned before.

However, the reason I bring this up, is because it was during 'The Messiah Conspiracy' that I developed the Irvine Method that this book is about.

At the time, I didn't call it that, in fact it was only during Chapter One of this book that I realised that I would have to give the process a name for the purpose of this book.

In the many books that have come since 'The Messiah Conspiracy', I have tried to repeat the experiences which drove me to write 'The Messiah Conspiracy', and I've discovered that it wasn't just a fluke. It *was* repeatable and work over and over again. That's why I am now writing about it and sharing it with you and others.

The process works.

It's incredible.

And life-changing, if you will allow it to be.

I can hear some of you saying, '*That's impossible! … you must have done some planning.*'

And perhaps you are a little correct… but just a little… and I will cover that in the second part of this chapter later – '*Plotter or Pantser Part Two*'.

The summary of this chapter is that you should just start the book as soon as you can.

Allow your subconscious to do the planning and plotting.

But TRUST that your subconscious *will* do it.

Another, perhaps more clever way of saying this, is, that once you've started, the book will write itself.

Which is not completely true, because books can't write.
You have to do the writing.
Which is the topic of the next chapter: Learn to Touch-Type.

Chapter 6

Learn To Touch-Type

Probably the most useful skill that any author or writer can learn is to touch-type,

Why?

Simply because, as you will learn throughout this book, it's all about getting your subconscious to write the book for you, through your conscious self.

The idea is that you sit down at your keyboard, start to type, and the text begins to appear on the page in front of you, fluidly, swiftly, as your subconscious-self flows through you, down your fingers, onto the keys, into your laptop and onto the 'page'.

Once you open up your creative channel, you want the words to flow as fast as you can think of them.

If you can successfully 'tap into' your creative flow, then your fingers become the conduit through which your book materialises, and your eyes and conscious brain provide the managerial oversight which ensures that you correct mistakes, don't skip lines, or that the text looks good on the page.

The last thing you want to do at this point is to continuously have to go back and correct mistakes. You want the writing to flllllllloooooooowwwwww.

Also, you don't want to continuously have to stop the creative flow while you fix the mistakes your conscious self has made.

Lastly, once the text begins to flow, you don't want to have to throttle it down or slow it up to the point that a big bottleneck of text, ideas and brilliant inspiration develops in your mind.

If that happens, you may get frustrated. Agitated. Annoyed. Fed-up.

And your finger that continuously pounds the 'backspace' and the 'delete' key will get worn out.

No.

That is not a good idea.

So, if I may, I would like to suggest that if you are serious about wanting to write a novel, then in the evenings or lunchtimes or mornings when you are not working on your book, then you start and continue to develop and work on 'touch-typing' skills for writing on a keyboard.

I could suggest that before you even start to write, that you spend some time training and raising your touch-typing skills to a decent level, but I'm worried that if I suggest that, some of the procrastinators and perfectionists in the audience will use this as an excuse to put off starting the book.

Hopefully, once you've read Chapter 9 below on visualisation and motivation, this won't be a problem. However, just in case, I would suggest that you do both in parallel.

Start the book.

And learn to type.

The good news is, obviously, that as you write your book, you will get better and better at it. Practice makes perfect, after all!

I won't recommend any particular course to you, simply because I haven't tried any out.

My uncle taught me how to touch-type when I was a child. He said it would be a life-skill and he was completely correct. I would perhaps recommend any parents among you to encourage your children to touch-type at some point. It will save them hours or days during their time as a student if they go to college, and will be a significant positive skill in their future workplace, wherever that is.

If you need help in choosing a way to learn then you can simply go online and type in 'Learn to Touch-Type' into your favourite internet browser, and then browse through the results you find.

Or, if you don't want to learn online, the method my uncle taught me years ago, was to draw four rows of circles on a piece of paper, and then fill in the letters within the circles in the same layout and format of your local keyboard to make a 'pretend' practice keyboard -different countries and languages have different layouts and symbols!

Once you've done this, memorise the layout of the letters row by row.

Position your fingers above the paper, and start practicing set lines of text, slowly instructing your fingers where to move to hit different letters.

The perfect sentence to use in most English-speaking countries is:

'The quick brown fox jumps over the lazy dog.'

Why?

Because it contains every letter of the English alphabet.

So, if you practice typing this on the piece of paper, at first with your eyes open, then with your eyes closed, you will learn where all the letters are on the keyboard.

Once this is done, perhaps even whilst you are watching TV, you can put your pretend paper keyboard on your lap on a tray, and practice typing words that the person on the television says. Or any word that comes into your mind.

Get your fingers moving.

When you are on a train, or a bus, or commuting to work, you can close your eyes and imagine the keyboard, and practice 'typing' in your mind's eye, moving your fingers in sympathy to your thoughts, perhaps tapping the fingers against your leg as you 'type' the words you imagine.

Once you've learned the position of the letters on the keyboard, you can then migrate to a real keyboard.

Perhaps sit in front of the TV with the keyboard on your lap.

I think you get the picture here… Practice makes perfect.

Slowly, over time, build up your speed.
L----e----a---r----n   t---o   t--y--p--e   f-a-s-t-e-r!

A last word of advice on this would be to make sure you use a keyboard which is big enough for your hand and your fingers.

If the keyboard on your device of choice is too small, buy a bigger keyboard and plug it into your device.

In order to type fast and correctly, your fingers must be comfortable and not fighting for space or banging into each other.

Otherwse youll continuiaonsly be making lotts of missstakees.

Sorry.

Chapter 7

Author Or Writer?

Some of you will love this chapter. For others it will make your head spin.

Did you know you could become an author without ever writing a book?

Or that some of the most famous authors you may have heard of don't write the books which make them famous?

When I first found this out, I can remember having arguments with my literary agent that it wasn't true… I insisted that authors were the people who wrote books.

It was only when I realised that the word author in some other languages literally equates to the concept of 'producer' that the penny dropped.

Basically, what this means is that whoever pulls together the content of a book, formats it and presents it as a book worthy of publication, then that person can be defined as the author. He/she creates the book, produces it and makes it happen.

And this is the interesting part: the author can take unpublished work written by other people, put it into a book, and then publish it, and then become the person whose name appears on the cover of the book.

Quite often the author will credit the writer or writers by including their name on the front cover somehow, but not always.

Recently I read a very well-known book where towards the end the author explained that most of the chapters were in fact written by an assistant.

That assistant's name was mentioned.

But it wasn't on the front cover, or in any way associated with the publication of the book.

This sounds unfair!

However, it is accepted practice.

Today, perhaps, it's even becoming more common, because the world of Independent Publishing has spawned a revolution in the way books are created, published and read.

You may not have realised it, but a growing number of authors are paying other people to write the contents of books for them. The model is that the 'author' commissions the work from 'writers' and pays them a set sum. The author then publishes and promotes the book, and pockets the money, or pays the debts that hence ensue.

So, why is this relevant to you?

Because, if becoming an author is your dream or is on your bucket list, then this approach provides another avenue you may not previously have thought about.

Personally, I think that you if follow the Irvine Method outlined in this book, you will want to write the book yourself. However, if following this process your head fills with ideas, which you then discover you can't do justice to in the actual writing, you could potentially consider paying someone else to turn your ideas into written text or content, which you then publish under your name.

The writer is happy because they were paid to write something – and writers love to write! – and you are happy because you have finally become an author!

It sounds crazy, but actually it isn't. It's just a different approach you may not be used to.

You may be surprised to learn that this isn't really a new thing, either.

In the past, many famous artists, some truly household names, often set up painting factories, where they paid other artists to paint works-of-art in a particular style, and when a painting was complete, the commissioning artist (the author of the painting) then picked up a paintbrush and painted his name in the corner of the canvas.

It's been happening for hundreds of years!

Just to be clear, I don't particularly like this model, but then again, I am a writer: I love to write.

I've been a writer for over twenty years.

I've only been an author for the past eight since my first book was published on Amazon.

Chapter 8

The Shape of the Book:

The Beginning, the End, the Middle.

We're close, very close, to being able to start your book. We've only two more things to sort out, perhaps three, and then you are ready to sit down, take a deep breath and start writing. Before that, you've got this chapter and the next to go through.

Which are perhaps two of the most important.

(Have I said that before?)

In this chapter we will look at the importance of asking your subconscious to give you the beginning, the end, and the middle of the book.

Key to this is that you ask your subconscious mind to do this, and that you don't try to do it yourself, consciously.

Before we move on though, for ease of reference and when referring to your subconscious, let's give it a name. How about SC? (Sub-Conscious?)

In the Irvine Method we trust 'SC' to come up with a brilliant story, of which, two of the most important parts are the beginning and the end.

I suggest you don't 'consciously' try to come up with something which you 'consciously' think is brilliant, but that you let SC do it for you.

What you must do, however, is to go through the exercise of asking SC to come up with a catchy beginning to the story that you have outlined in Chapter 3, and wait for this beginning to pop into your mind.

You should stress to yourself and SC that this beginning needs to be immediately interesting. It has to 'catch' your readers quickly, and compel them to read on. In many ways, the first few paragraphs and pages have to be the best part of the book. They rank second only in importance to those last few pages at the end of the book which must leave the reader begging for more.

It may be that SC gives you a couple of different suggested beginnings to the book, each of which pop into your head whilst walking, or swimming, or sleeping and dreaming… or in the bath, causing you to jump up and shout 'Eureka!' before slipping on the soap and falling back down into the tub!

Wherever that inspired beginning is revealed to you, once you're happy with it, nod to yourself, accept it, and then ask the next question.

"How does the book finish?"

For poor old SC, I think this is the hardest question of all. For SC to be able to answer it, SC has to have a very vague idea of how the story will weave its way to the ending. At this stage your conscious self may not be informed of that part, but that will come in due course.

For now, all you need to ask SC to provide you with, is a *target* ending.

A way in which you feel that the book and its story will end.

In my latest thriller book, which I am just writing at the moment, I started off with the idea that a character would be pushed off the top of a tall building. It would be a fairly dramatic opening scene.

I imagined that at the end of the book, the serial killer responsible for the murder described in the first chapter would be surrounded by police, and he would then blow himself up.

A fairly dramatic ending.

In other words, I now had a beginning – an opening scene – and an ending, the final scene.

Once these were available, I now had all the tools necessary that would permit me to sit down and start writing: I had a title, a theme, a high-level description of the story and plot, a beginning scene, and an ending, and the name and profession of the main character.

Putting all of these together gives the writer the skeleton of the book. Admittedly, there is quite a lot to flesh out, but that's the fun part. And that's what SC will help you to do every day when you sit down to write the next chapter.

Perhaps, at this stage, I should suggest a few more rules to the Irvine Method:

1: You are allowed to change your mind about the opening scene.

2: You are allowed to change your mind about the closing scene.

Generally, once you've made up your mind, you'll find you won't have to, but I think that if you feel that you must, you can.

The other purpose of having a good opening scene that I haven't mentioned yet, is that it's not just for your readers, it's also for *you*!

I believe that you really should be excited about starting to write the book.

When a writer sits down to cast those first few words onto the empty canvas where he will come to toil and sweat (sounds dramatic) day after day for the next couple of months (not years!), he/she should be excited, enthused, full of adrenaline.

Starting a book is a big thing!

(Finishing it is even bigger…)

So, I suggest that once SC has popped a suggested beginning into your mind which you really like and have accepted… then you take a few more days to walk around, go swimming, … whatever it is you do to relax… and use that time to ponder just how you feel about that beginning.

It may be that after the initial excitement dies down, you decide that the beginning is not strong enough.

If so, don't be scared: tell SC to go away and come up with another suggestion. And then ponder that one too.

The important thing is that you must be excited about your opening scene.

After all, if you're not, why should your readers be?

Once you're very comfortable and enthusiastic about whatever beginning you've settled on, then start to play with the idea.

Imagine your first words.

Start to imagine what those first paragraphs will look like on the pages of the book.

See the pages with your own eyes.

Imagine touching the pages with your fingers.

Consider what it would be like to hold your first book when it's finished.

Now, everything I just said about the beginning of the book… do the same for the ending too.

Regardless of whether you are going to be an Indie Author or published via traditional channels, it's important to consider how the reader will feel once they finish the book.

Ideally, you want the reader to be exhausted from not sleeping for the past few days because he/she hasn't been able to put down the book since picking it up… and when they get to the final few pages of the book, and finally devour those last few words, the first thing you want them to say is … "Wow!" (or something to that effect.)

In other words, you want the end of the book to deliver on the promise that has been built up during the course of the book.

The last thing a reader wants is an ending that does not deliver.

Unless that is… you want the book to lead into a sequel which the reader then feels absolutely compelled to purchase!

So, focus on the ending. Make sure you are happy with it and that it excites you just as much as the beginning does. And then go with it!

(Just remember… you CAN change the ending, if you feel you must, right up to the moment you are about to write it!)

There is one further point we need to consider about the shape of the book.

It's called 'The Middle'.

In the Irvine Method, there are three basic navigation points for each novel you write.

You start with a beginning. You end on the ending.

And somewhere in between, about half-way through, you establish the middle.

Now… this is actually quite important. For the following reason…

Not only does The Middle act as a wonderful guide to keep the story on track, but it also helps regulate how many words you are going to write.

Remember my own personal disaster which turned into 300,000 words? One reason this happened was because as I cruised my way through the book, I didn't know where the middle should be. I didn't have a 'target' which pinpointed the middle of the book, and consequently I had nothing to caution me when I steamed towards the theoretical number of words where 'The Middle' should have occurred. I just kept writing.

So, I suggest this: having established an opening scene, and a closing scene, you next ask SC to conjure up the scene that appears in the middle of the book.

Once you have accepted a scene that SC suggests, when you then write the book, you need to continuously be aware that any action which should take place as you move towards the middle of the book, does indeed take place before the middle.

As the middle of the book comes thundering towards you, you should allow small, tiny, alarm bells to start ringing in your head.

If SC doesn't pay attention to them and start delivering up the correct content for the chapters you write as get you closer and closer, then you go for a walk and have some serious words with SC!

(Note: By this point I am not encouraging any of you to develop schizophrenic tendencies... SC is actually *you*... so don't start imagining another you, if that makes sense!)

The bottom line is this: don't overshoot the middle with any action that should take place before the middle, and try as best you can to hit the middle of the book with the target scene that you think should occur there.

Again, this is not a firm rule. As the story develops and evolves, the exact position of a middle scene may vary, but what is very, very important, is that at all times you are aware of just how much you have written, and where what you have written is, in relation to the potential middle and ending of that story.

The good news is that having established a beginning, an end, and then now also a middle, SC will, unbeknownst to Conscious You (CY from now on!), now start to develop the plots that take you to the middle of that first half of the book – i.e. a quarter of the way through the book - and likewise, the middle of the latter half of the book. Etc.

Although you may not have realised it yet, by doing the above, CY and SC have now started to 'frame' the story.

You begin to develop a sense of what needs to happen within the story, and by when, and in the back of your mind, and arguably at the forefront of SC's, a time-line of events begins to appear.

As the story begins to unfold as you write it, you will picture and develop a feeling for when different parts of the emerging plot should happen, and how those happenings, then affect other events in the book.

Slowly, the book will develop structure.

And the plot will, quite literally, thicken.

By now I hope you are starting to feel a little excited about what you are going to do. And achieve.

You ARE going to write a book.

It will be amazing!

In the next chapter, we're going to put this all on auto-pilot.

We're going to learn an incredibly powerful visualisation technique that will quite literally turbo charge your desire to write a book, and give you the confidence and willpower to do it.

If you follow the guidance provided in the coming pages and practice everything as suggested, then you will emerge from the next chapter as an author or writer who is determined to produce your book, and who is committed and motivated to make it happen!

Warning: Don't read the next chapter if you don't want to write or be an author! Once you have read it, there's no going back!

Gulp.

Now go to the next step.

Chapter 9

Motivate Yourself To Write

(with an incredibly powerful Visualisation Technique!)

WARNING: THIS CHAPTER IS FOR ADULTS ONLY: IT USES POWERFUL VISUALISATION TECHNIQUES NOT APPROPRIATE FOR MINORS.

Many people have the desire to write a book, and some come up with a good idea, but few people actually do it. Why not? The reason is that most people are not actually motivated enough to put in the time, or they are full of self-doubt and don't believe it is possible for them to actually achieve their dream. They spend so much time busy with their negative thoughts, doubting themselves, worrying about how they can write the book, or doubting that SC will be able to help them write it, that they never ever start the first line.

In this chapter we are going to change all that.

I am going to teach you a mental trick that will generate an incredible source of powerful, internal motivation that will literally have you champing at the bit to go and write the book of your dreams.

You will feel a constant drive and desire to go and write.

To work on your book.

To make your book a reality so that you can feel it in your hands.

To touch it.

Smell it.

Make your book *real*!

We will take away any self-doubt you may have and we will help you believe that you can and will write the book.

Not only will you believe you can, but you will *know* that you can.

Because in your mind's eye you will have seen the finished product and touched it already!

Let me add that this powerful trick, once you learn it, is not only restricted to the creation of books. You can apply it to any goal or task you may have.

For some of you – and this is not a joke – this chapter could change your life.

So how can this be done? And how do I know it works? I know it because I use this trick on myself to produce all my books.

Before I tell you how it's done though, I have to confess that it's not actually a trick. It's a real thing, based upon the science of Neuro Linguistic Programming (NLP), and is based upon the NLP techniques developed by the genius Dr. Richard Bandler.

You can go and read about him later on, but for now, I just want you to know that this will work, if you give yourself permission for it to work.

This bit is important. You have to first give yourself permission for it to work, and you have to be twilling to give it a go!

It's nothing ominous, or strange, but at first it sounds a little daft.

Only when you do it, will you begin to realise that it actually works.

So, are you ready to give it a shot?
Ready to begin?

If you are, do the following. In order.

You will need to read the following several times before you do this, because you can't read the instructions and perform the actions at the same time. But once you've got the picture of what you are going to do, put down the book, and go and do it. Or perhaps you can ask your partner to read the text below to you whilst you are sitting or lying down in your preferred, chosen place of relaxation. If that's possible, your partner should read it to you slowly, in a relaxed and soothing voice.

PART ONE: Set aside thirty minutes of your time to give to yourself. To treat yourself. To reward yourself. To relax. Unwind. And to see your future.

PART TWO: When you have the time, take yourself to your happy place. Your favourite seat in the house. Your bedroom, Your garden. Somewhere, anywhere, where you know you will be able to relax. In peace. And. Quiet.

PART THREE: When you are there, in your chosen space, allow yourself to sit down or lie down. To relax. To feel good about yourself.

PART FOUR: Once you are seated, or are lying down, close your eyes. Take five deep slow breaths. Breathe in. Breathe out slowly. Relax.

Repeat this last part three times.

PART FIVE: Now, think of the most beautiful or relaxing place you have ever been, or the place you would like to be right now, if you are not already there. Picture it in your mind. Add colour to the picture. Imagine any sounds that you might hear if you were there. Make it more real.

Now imagine a flight of steps, going down from where you are now, to the place you want to be. Leading down to where you are most at peace and relaxed. Your favourite place.

Imagine five steps. In your mind's eye I want you to imagine you are going to put out a foot, and step down to the next step below. Breathe in. Deeply. Exhale slowly, and *now step down*, go deeper, from where you are now to the next level below.

With each step down and with each breath in and out, you will feel more relaxed.

Getting ready now, preparing to feel more relaxed, and more content, and more able to learn new things, *now step forward and go down*, going deeper down to the next level of peace, and contentment.

Good. With each step down, you will feel more relaxed. More content. More peaceful.

Breathe in and feel more relaxed. Relax more with each breath you take.

Now, put out your foot and *step down again* to the next level of *deeper relaxation* and feeling good about yourself. Breathe in. Breathe out. You feel more relaxed. More peaceful. *Ready to learn* how to *motivate* yourself to achieve your dream of writing your book.

Now smile and go down even deeper, *stepping down now to the next level*. With each breath feel yourself becoming more relaxed. More in tune with yourself. More content. Happier. Relaxed...

With one more step to go, *step down now* to the next level, going deeper, down into a more comfortable and fulfilling sense of relaxation and contentment. Ready to learn and excited about knowing that your dream of becoming a writer will soon come true.

And now, once you have finally arrived, down at the bottom of your five steps, in the place you feel most at home and most comfortable, *RELAX*.

Imagine looking around yourself, in the place where you now are. The place you like to be. Where you always feel relaxed. And happy.

Allow yourself to feel good. To feel amazing.

And *RELAX*.

PART SIX: Empty your mind. There's no rush. Take your time. Just relax. Enjoy being in your happy place. When you are feeling comfortable, and ready to move on to fill yourself with motivation that will enthuse and drive you forward to write a book, then continue to the next step.

PART SEVEN: Now that you are feeling relaxed and at peace, I would like you to build a mental picture in your mind of what your finished book will look like when it is created and done.
Build the picture.

Imagine your book somewhere in front of you.
Picture it.
See it.

See the book in your mind's eye, the name of the book on the front cover, in big letters, and your name on the top or bottom of the cover.

Imagine it. See it. Picture it. Your book. Your name. Your title on the book.

Now let me ask you a question: when you do this, is this mental image you have constructed, small or large?
How far away from you is the book?
Do you imagine it far away, or close by, just in front of you?
So far so good. Now, still with your eyes closed, I want you to do the following.
First, if you picture the book in your mind in black and white, I want you to force yourself to add some colour.
In your mind, make the picture on the book cover that you see, *brighter*, and *more* vivid.
See the *title get larger*, your name more prominent.
Next, I want you to imagine the *size* of the book getting *bigger.*
In your mind's eye, see your hands reach out to the edge of the book.
See your fingers touch the edge of the book and bring it closer to you.
Pull the book towards you.
See the image of your book getting larger.
With both hands on the edge of the book, now bring it even closer to you.

Make it larger.

Imagine it now, not far away, but right there, in front of you. *Only just in front of you.*

In bright colours. Your name easy to read on the cover. The title you have chosen for the book, bright and distinctive.

The book is now *so close* that you can reach out and *feel* it. You can open the book and turn the pages. Whenever you want.

The book is so close that it's real. It's there. You can see it before you. Finished. Complete!

The book that YOU wrote!

Imagine it.

Remember it.

Feel what it is like to be a *successful author.*

Remember this sensation.

Smile.

Feel good about yourself.

Congratulate yourself.

In your mind's eye, see yourself reaching out and touching the book which *you* have written.

Capture that incredible feeling you may have, how happy and content you feel at this time, because you have achieved your goal. You are a writer!

Feel good.

Remember that sensation.

Remember it.

Breathe deeply.

In, out.

And relax.

Breathe in.

Breathe out.

PART EIGHT: Now slowly, imagine yourself preparing to walk back up the stairs to where you came from, but this time, keeping the image of the book which you will write, fresh in your mind.

Back up the stairs.

One step at a time.

Now step up to the next level, from five to four, and remember how happy you felt when you could touch your own book. Keep the picture of your book fresh in your mind.

Step up again to the level above. From four to three. Breathing in and out, remembering that your dream of writing a book will now come true.

Step up again to the next level above. From three to two. Think about the image of your book just in front of you. So close. You can almost touch it.

Step back up from two to one. Imagine still the title of your book, so bright and vivid.

Now return up that final step, from one to where you started, but now full of enthusiasm and determination to make your dream come true and to write your book. Still able to picture the book in your mind. So real. Just in front of you. Its cover bright, vivid and real.

You are now motivated to write that book. Soon. Very soon. Until it is finished and ready to publish!

Your book. Complete. And finished.

Now, slowly, open your eyes.

And smile.

Feeling good about yourself and what you have seen and learnt.

Breathe deeply.

PART NINE: Take a moment.

Then think of your book.

Once again, think of your book.

Imagine it.

This time, how far away from you is the book in your mind's eye? Can you touch it? How bright are the colours on the cover?

If you can see the book in full colour, and it's almost there, just in front of you, so close you can almost touch it, then you are ready to go to the next chapter! Now fully motivated. Determined to make your book happen. Excited and happy about the journey you are just about to begin to become a writer. Very close to realising your dream and making it come true!

If the book you see is not right there just in front of you, not large and in colour, then allow yourself to go back to the beginning of this chapter and repeat it all. Slowly.

There's no rush.

Each time you do it, the book you imagine will be a little bigger, closer, more vivid.

More real.

Don't worry if you have to repeat the process a few times until you feel you're ready. That's perfectly fine. And very relaxing!

PART TEN: When you are feeling good, and relaxed, and you can almost 'touch' the book and you can easily see it or conjure up a large colour picture of it in your mind when you close your eyes, or even with your eyes open, then turn to the next chapter!

Chapter 10

Making A Start!

The time has come!

Now is the time for you to sit down at your laptop or device, to arrange your chair and your keyboard so that you're comfortable, and to take a deep breath.

Open up your word document, or Scrivener, or whatever other writing or word processing application you chose. Pen and paper? Quill?

Move your cursor to the top of the page in the middle – perhaps by formatting it by centring it using Home/Paragraph/Centre or Control E – and then type the following magic words: 'Chapter One'.

Now you have a decision to make. Your first writing decision within the book.

Are you going to give each chapter a title?

If so, now is the time for your first piece of creative writing: what are you going to call it?

Take two minutes, no longer, write something down and then move on.

Left justify the text and move to the first word of the first paragraph of your first book.

Are you nervous?

Are you excited?

Both are good feelings.

But now is the time to move forward.

Start writing!

At this point you should have an idea of how you are going to start the first chapter. You should also have an idea of what it is that you are wanting to cover.

If you don't, just remember everything you've thought of so far in the chapters before.

The important part is to remember that SC is right there with you. Urging you on. Whispering in your ear what you should write next.

Trust yourself.

Believe that the words will come.

And they will.

Don't worry if you write a page and then decide you should edit it. Editing comes later. If you have never written a book before, the reality is that you will take a while to develop your own style, or 'find your voice', as some people put it.

Writing is a skill. You have to develop and hone it.

Few of us are masters at it straight away.

But don't be afraid to experiment. Play with the words and sentences and find a way of writing that you not only think the readers will enjoy, but which you are also comfortable with adopting.

In this book I am not setting out to teach you how to write a masterpiece, or what makes a good literary work of art. All I can say is that a lot of that is personal taste.

I for one, am no literary genius.

I have to admit that my writing style is not the most loved by everyone.

I start sentences with 'But', 'Because' and 'And'.

My sentences are short.

Sometimes very.

My Grammar is terrible.

And I make hundredds of speling mistakes.

But, over the years I have developed a way of writing that I quite enjoy and which my 'fans' – that's an interesting word! – seem to enjoy. People seem to find my 'voice' refreshing and different. Not everyone. Yet enough to make it all worthwhile.

So, be bold, make a start. Experiment. Have fun.

Start typing away.

Begin your journey and good luck!

Chapter 11

Writing Each Chapter As A Mini-book

In the last chapter I confessed that I am not an expert who knows how to 'write'. I have not yet written a masterpiece, or a book which is so beautiful that it makes people cry.

I'm reluctant to give readers any advice on how to 'write'.

Personally, one of my own goals is to improve the way I write, to get better and better, and perhaps one day write a book which is critically acclaimed.

To learn with every book I write.

So, that said, and given that I don't want to preach to you on the skills of writing, is there anything I can suggest to you about the mechanics of writing a book? Can I share any thoughts with you on how to physically make a book a page-turner, or to keep the book engaging, fresh, and exciting, throughout?

I've thought about this, and I believe there are perhaps two pieces of advice I can give here.

The first of these is to write each chapter as a mini-story in its own right.

Each chapter, I believe, should contain a small story, and should end on a cliffhanger or a question which can only be resolved by reading the next chapter.

By doing this the reader never gets the excuse to put the book down. If they are enjoying your writing, they will find your book very frustrating in a very positive sense: they will continuously be starting the next chapter and hoping to find some form of resolution or pause in the action so that they can finally eat, or sleep, or go for a walk, but the trick is not to let them.

Don't let them go to sleep at night, by striving to make each of your chapters so compelling that they MUST READ JUST ONE MORE CHAPTER to see what happens next... and then the next chapter... and the next!

The second piece of advice I could possibly offer you, if you will let me, is to suggest that each chapter should be about five pages long. Not too long, and not too short.

Long enough to keep the action in the novel moving forward, but short enough to make it possible for a reader to digest a chapter in a short journey on a bus whilst commuting to work, for example.

Short enough to keep the reader moving rapidly through the book from one chapter to another, and giving the reader a sense of momentum.

Short enough to keep the tension in the book building from chapter to chapter.

But long enough to contain enough action to deliver each next component of the story.

Although the main point is that each chapter should deliver one core building block or piece of the overall story-jigsaw-puzzle that you need to build throughout the book, it may also contain a few smaller, minor points.

You start the chapter, construct a vehicle for delivering the next point of the storyline, and then once that's done you prepare to cut-and-run: but not before you drop the cliffhanger, teaser or question that makes the reader move to the next chapter and alludes to the next piece of the jigsaw puzzle!

Never be tempted to drag a chapter out unnecessarily. Be ruthless.

To recap on this chapter then... Each chapter should:

- Be about five pages.
- Deliver one main 'point' of the story.
- Provide a teaser pointing to the next chapter.

Then you're done. Move on. Next chapter.

(Actually, now's the time to move onto Chapter 12)

Chapter 12

Plotter Or Pantser: How To Write The Book (Part Two)

Welcome to the second part of the extended chapter on 'Plotter or Pantser'.

If you can remember we previously talked about the ability to write by the seat of your pants without great amounts of detailed planning, as opposed to spending months or years making detailed plans for every aspect of the plot and the characters that appear in the story.

My strong encouragement was to just sit down and start writing - and to let SC plan and write the book for you whilst you are sleeping, walking, talking or doing something completely different.

Even when you are asleep SC is active, dreaming, thinking, paying attention to what's going on, and keeping you safe.

Have you ever wondered why you don't fall off the side of the bed? It's because SC knows your position on the mattress, and when you come to the edge of it, SC spots the fact that a limb is hanging over the edge, and either makes you roll back onto the bed, or monitors your position so you don't go further over the edge.

SC is always active. In other words, SC always has your back, and is constantly working on your behalf!

So, with SC on your side, you can be both a Plotter and a Pantser: you do the Pantsing, and SC does the Plotting!

It sounds ideal! And it almost is.

What I didn't tell you completely upfront in Part One, however, is that the Plotting-Pantsing thing you have going on between you and SC is actually a 'partnership'.

You have to work together to get the whole book written.

Also, SC doesn't suddenly download the whole book into your conscious brain in one instant, moment of time.

What actually happens is that SC writes the book through your conscious self one chapter at a time, and only upon demand.

Perhaps explaining it better in another way, effectively, you are the manager of the partnership, supervising what jobs SC has to do, and telling SC when it has to deliver on or complete the tasks you set it!

Also, whereas SC does most of the plot setting and character development, you have significant input into steering the direction of travel and setting the pace of the book. If something suddenly happens when you are writing the book – like when the main character was suddenly killed off in my book *The Messiah Conspiracy* – you could, if you want, ignore that development or reject it, and force SC to come up with an alternative.

Now we come to the crux of the matter in the Plotter-Pantser relationship that you will have going on between your subconscious creative self and your conscious self - the discussion of how you go about writing all the individual chapters in the book.

Some of you may have spotted the fact that until now I have only suggested how you write the first chapter, the last chapter and the middle chapter.

"But what about all the rest?" I hear some of you asking!

Good question. In fact, excellent question.

And this is the answer: previously, we talked about how the goal was to end each chapter on a cliffhanger, or a question that can only be resolved by reading on further.

The cliffhanger or the question raised at the end of a previous chapter can therefore act as the guide what you write about in the next chapter, where you resolve in the *new* chapter the question raised in the *last*.

Sometimes, however, when you have several storylines developing and running throughout the book in parallel, it is possible that the 'next' chapter may not follow on directly from the previous one; it could be the next chapter relates to a prior preceding chapter.

In such cases, when the next chapter to be written doesn't actually automatically connect with the chapter directly before, you may have to resort to going for one of your walks, going swimming, taking a break, or having a bath, etc., and simply asking SC what happens in the next chapter?

As you become more experienced at writing, you develop the ability to maintain a small list of questions and actions that need to be resolved or occur in the coming chapters, and to keep this list forefront in your mind.

Whenever you have a moment away from writing, you will find yourself thinking about what's on that list, and considering how to write about it, or connect different items together.

You begin to ask yourself how to write about and connect or create elements of the story, without even really realising that's what you are doing! It could be that SC begins to take the lead and start prompting you to think about certain things, instead of the other way around.

Whichever way it happens, I find that personally, for me, the best way to initiate the whole thought process about *"what should I write about in the next chapter?"* is to go swimming.

After a couple of lengths of swimming, my mind goes blank, and I can block out the rest of the world and focus on what's going to happen in the next chapter.

I ask questions, think about what's on the list I just mentioned above, and wait for answers to pop into my mind.

After I've finished swimming I go to the sauna, and very often, while I am relaxing in the sauna with a blank mind, the answers to the current questions I have been asking just pop into my head. Swimming and the sauna both work for me. For you it might be golf. Or skiing. Or walking... It could be one of many different ways where you manage to relax, block out your other worries and thoughts, and start to imagine the next scenes in your book.

I think it's important to say here that you approach and do this chapter by chapter. Generally, I tend to write one or two chapters a day, so I get plenty of time in the morning, afternoon, evening, or overnight to think about and plan what will appear in the next chapter when I get a chance to sit down and let it be written.

Remember, Rome wasn't built in a day.

Tomorrow is the first day in the rest of your life.

A book appears chapter by chapter. One page after the next.

Good. Excellent! So now we know, in advance before we sit down at the keyboard, what the main points are that will need to be covered in each of the next chapters you will write.

You approach the book, one chapter at a time.

Well, almost.

There are two exceptions.

Firstly, as you get towards the middle of the book, you have to start considering how many pages you have to go before you hit that magic middle point. You then have to translate that number of pages into a number of anticipated chapters.

And then, you need to start thinking about the various plot points that may need to be covered or resolved before you get to the middle point of the book.

One way of doing this it to consider where you are now in the plot that is developing, where you need to be to reach the middle point, and then to work backwards in your mind from the action that takes place in the middle to where you are now.

You may then come up with a shortlist of actions, sequences or events that need to happen to the characters before the middle point of the book can be reached. This short list of actions may then dictate what the content of the next few chapters has to be.

Likewise, when you are on the home straight and heading towards the end of the book, you need to do the same.

Consider where you are now, where you need to be at the end of the book, what events have to take place before the end so that the end can be reached, and then work backwards to generate a list of actions you need to write about in the coming chapters…

Phew…!

Take a breath…

So, what have we learned in this chapter?
(Hopefully something!…?)

My intention is that you would learn that a book is built chapter by chapter. Not instantly, all at once, but gradually. From one scene to another.

This is important, because it means that in the interplay between your conscious self and your subconscious 'creative' self, you do not need to consider everything all at the same time. You only need to worry about one chapter at a time.

Worrying about one chapter, is far more manageable than worrying about fifty, or a hundred chapters! (How long is your book going to be?)

In the next chapter we'll look very briefly at how to make each chapter come alive using the power of visualisation which is at the heart of the Irvine Method.

Chapter 13

Building Colour And Detail Into The Book:

Use The Power Of Visualisation!

To be frank, I am not a very good writer. My 'prose' is very clumsy, my speling is terrible, and my Grammar ain't good. It's awful. My books could probably all do with more editing to spot the mistakes I haven't noticed.

However, many of the two million people who have downloaded my books seem to enjoy them, and a lot of them give me a similar compliment, which goes something like this:

"Your books are like little films that run in my mind. I can see the action and feel what the characters are experiencing!"

I take that as a great compliment.

It also makes me smile because it means that I have achieved what I really have set out to do.

When I write, I try to describe in as much detail as I can what I see in my own mind.

When SC – my subconscious self – guides me to write a scene, I try to see in my mind's eye anything that the characters in that scene would be doing, and then to describe it.

If for example, the scene has a character walking into a room, looking round the room and then doing something in the room, I force myself to imagine the door, the room on the other side of the door, and its contents and orientation. I then force myself to experience the sensation of the character walking into the room, and describe through his eyes what they see. Then, if the character does something in that room, I try to summarise the action.

I try to make a little video of the action in my mind and describe it to the best of my ability, so that someone else could also experience that scene just as I had done.

There is also something else.

I try to write in a way that stimulates readers' senses.

In any scene, I try to imagine and then describe what a character may see, hear, smell or feel, describing in as much detail as possible, what the sensations are that they feel.

Some people are visual, some are auditory.

So, if you want to describe a bright, sunny day where the hero of the story walks through a forest in autumn, crushing the red, bright yellow and green autumnal leaves beneath his black shoes into the brown earth, you might want to pepper the text with references that could stimulate their sense of sight. Do you get the picture?

For people who respond well to the description of sounds - who are 'auditory' in nature - the same walk through the forest should emphasise the dry leaves crunching beneath the hero's feet as he runs through the trees. It's raining, and the sound of raindrops dripping from the wet leaves onto the ground is soon drowned out by the crashing thunder which explodes across the sky.

Do you hear where I'm coming from?

Lastly, some people respond well to descriptions of touch. For them, you may write about the crinkly dry leaves, or the rough, ragged bark on the trees, or the slimy moss on the wet stones. These people are described as being kinesthetic.

Of course, you can't tell what type of person a reader may be, so you can't target your book to your readers individually. Instead, you alternate between them in your writing, and strive to stimulate as many of our human senses as possible.

I'm perhaps also guilty of describing lots of movement in my novels. The characters are always doing something, and I think I write my books from the perspective of an invisible reporter who is constantly following the characters around just a metre behind them.

Perhaps one last tip, from my perspective, if I may.

I find it rather odd, but I am often told that my characters are very real. People can really identify with them, and they can picture them very well.

This is rather curious because I never really describe my characters at all.

I seldom say what colour hair they have, how big they are, or what clothes they wear.

I do this deliberately.

My characters are basically blank canvases onto which my readers can paint their own interpretations of who they are. In general, I try not to force my readers to think of characters in any particular way.

The result is that an awful lot of my readers think that I have described them very well indeed.

In fact, what is happening here is that the 'SC' in all of my readers is getting involved.

When a reader reads my books, their SC is whispering into their mind just what that SC sees or feels. And the reader accepts it.

Effectively, I am harnessing the power of my readers' imaginations (their SCs) to do my job for me!

Thankfully my readers all have vivid imaginations, and I get given all the credit!

I thank you all.

Chapter 14

Overcoming Problems By Looking Backwards Not Forwards

Writing a book can be a very daunting task. Even before you first sit down at the keyboard and stare at that blank page - a vast chunk of white space glowing ominously at you on the screen - onto which you are meant to type reams of wonderful words that will make people laugh, cry or bite their nails with the tension you create, the whole thing can be pretty scary.

Some people – who are not using the Irvine Method for writing – will never get past the first page. For them it will be like standing on the edge of the Atlantic Ocean, their shoes, off, their trousers turned up, and their socks in their pockets, and wondering how they will ever cross the sea from Scotland to America. The space between the beginning of the book and the end just seems so vast, and without any knowledge of how they can possibly navigate their way across, they just stare at the waves for hours, then just put their shoes and socks back on, and go to the pub instead.

With the Irvine Method, it's all very different. We have broken down the process of writing a book into steps, each of which is manageable. I've tried to show you how to approach each step, and I've tried to take the pressure of your writer's shoulders by convincing you that most of the hard graft will actually be done by SC – your subconscious self – when you are not even aware that it is happening.

If I haven't yet managed to convince you about the capability of your mind to do wonderful things for you, I've got one more idea about how to convince you of this.

Apparently, according to the answer I just found from googling my question on the internet, the human body has around 37.2 TRILLION cells in it.

That is, officially, quite a lot.

When you are healthy, and not in pain, most of us simply live our lives without even thinking about our bodies, our skeletons, our muscles, organs, blood vessels, or finger nails.

Yet, without us even sparing a momentary thought for it, our nails grow, our hair grows, our heart beats, our lungs give us air and help produce energy for our muscles to move, grow and repair, our organs keep us alive and moving. They flush out the toxins we are continuously filling our bodies with, even though we know it's bad for us. We talk to each other, processing sounds and visual stimulations into meanings and experiences which we memorise and often treasure.

We live.

We enjoy life.

We have ideas.

We create things.

We solve problems.

We do our jobs and earn money.

And almost all this time, the one thing that manages all aspects of all these processes - millions of processes that take place simultaneously and never stop, and of which we are never *CONSCIOUS* - is our *SUB*-Conscious.

So, given that your SUB-conscious has already got so much to do, what's the problem with just chucking in the small, tiny, miniscule little task of writing the next *War and Peace*, on top of all it's already got to do?

Actually, for your SC, it's not that big a job.

Just trust it to do it, and it will be done.

However, even though I say this, and even though most of you will believe it, others of you might *want* to believe it but still have a few hiccups along the way.

So, for those of you in that category, and perhaps anyone else who wants to learn this new mental trick so you can apply it to your private life in a million different ways when needed, can I share with you a novel little idea on how to overcome problems?

Basically, the issue that I want to help you overcome is this: sometimes, in life, when you face a problem, the issue seems so huge, so insurmountable, or so complex, that you feel overwhelmed. You give up trying to overcome the problem before you even start to try, because it just seems so ... daunting.

When facing a huge question, or task, you might not have the faintest idea of where to begin, or how to start to go about finding an answer. How should you tackle a problem? What needs to be done to overcome it?

You don't know what questions to ask, because you don't really know how to quantify the problem. Is there just one big task, or a million small tasks? What questions do you need to ask?

Imagine, once again, you are standing at the edge of the ocean in the UK, and all you know is that you want to get to America. All you have is a pair of shoes and the clothes you stand in.

For many, the problem of 'how' you might get to America is so overpowering that you just can't cope. Your brain can't compute the questions, because you don't know which questions to ask.

You are faced with a barrier, a wall of uncertainty and vagueness, and the wall seems so tall that you can't figure out how to get over it.

We stand in front of that barrier or wall, look up at it and tremble.

And give up.

Let me teach you another approach.

It's a very simple, yet very powerful technique or 'trick' that you can use to solve many, many different types of problems you may face in your life.

It also goes hand-in-hand with the visualisation technique I taught you in Chapter 9.

Here's how it works.

Should you ever face a seemingly insurmountable problem, or task (like writing a book!), I want to imagine that instead of facing the problem from the front of it, that you are looking at it from the other side.

I want you to IMAGINE, to PICTURE IN YOUR MIND that you have ALREADY OVERCOME THE PROBLEM, that you have COMPLETED THE TASK - whatever task that is - and that you are looking backwards into your past, across the task you have completed, to where you started your journey.

First, I want to you sense what it feels like to have completed the task.

Imagine that you have already succeeded.

The task is behind you.

The work is complete.

The job is done.

Remember that feeling.

Next, I want you to ask yourself a question: how did you overcome the problem and get it done?
How did you approach the task, and complete it?
How did you succeed?

Remember, in your mind's eye, that you have already *completed* the task. You have already overcome any problem that you might have faced before. But you *have* overcome it.

How?

Ask yourself what you did? How the problem was overcome?
Was that huge, enormous problem that you faced before, actually just one problem, or many smaller problems put together?
If so, what were they, and HOW DID YOU OVERCOME them?

Remember, believe that you have done it!
For example, in your mind's eye, you may now be standing at the top of the Empire State Building, having successfully made it to America. Or you may have written a book, had it published, and now you are sipping cocktails under that tree in the Caribbean working on your next book.

So, how did you get to America, and how did you write that book and get it published?

It's not, "How WILL I get to America?" or "How WILL I write this book and get it published?"
It's "How DID I get to America? Or "How DID I write the book?"

One word is different in the question you ask yourself, but the effect is phenomenal.

In the first question, you were overcome with the task, and your sub-conscious did not know how to FRAME the question. You never really tasked it with anything to do. You never gave it a problem to solve, because you couldn't FRAME the problem and break it down. In your imagination you just saw a wall. You didn't know how thick it was, or even if there were other walls behind it. How many walls (or problems) did you really need to overcome?

In the second question, you are asking your mind to start from a very different base-point. You are asking how you succeeded. You have programmed yourself to believe that you have already succeeded. There is no question of failure. You have not failed. You *have succeeded.*

You then ask your subconscious-creative-self to go away and think about how this was done.

Bingo!

A few days later, or weeks, or months, depending upon the size of the task/problem you have completed, or the scale of the achievement, your subconscious self will start feeding you answers as to just HOW you did it.

It will detail how you got from the start of the journey to where you imagined yourself at the end of the journey. It will detail the different stages you may have to go through to get there, breaking the journey down into smaller problems, and then detailing or suggesting how you got over those smaller issues.

With the benefit of visualised hindsight, SC will tell you how many walls you had to climb over, how thick those walls were, and how you did it.

Sometimes it will suggest solutions which are so obvious you will kick yourself.

"How did I get over the wall?" your conscious self may ask.

"You borrowed a ladder." SC might reply.

Turning to the example of the book, in the earlier chapter I asked you to imagine that you were touching or holding the finished product to generate real motivation and belief in yourself that you could achieve the task of writing that book.

I asked you to imagine that you had done it.

In response, SC would then later help you with all the small serial tasks of writing that book, chapter by chapter.

Occasionally, whilst you are writing the book, you may come up against some small challenges or problems which are either real or imagined.

You can use the above technique to overcome both.

Sometimes the 'problem' appears in the book, where a character has to do something, seemingly impossible, but to progress you have to come up with a way to describe how the character does the impossible.

Mentally, for a while, you consider this from the 'front' of the problem. You face the problem. You get nowhere.

So, you switch viewpoints. In your mind's eye you imagine that you (your character) is standing on the other side of the problem looking back. You ask SC to figure out and tell you just exactly how you did overcome the problem and achieve what needed to be done.

Bingo.

SC soon pops an answer into your head suggesting how you or your character did it. (It may be soon afterwards, or a few days later, but generally, it always works!)

Alternatively, the 'problem' you may encounter whilst writing the book may be a real one.

For example, your Wi-Fi has just stopped working and you can't get access to the internet to do some vital research which you need to do in order to write your next scene and make it more realistic.

You become really frustrated and angry!

So, you imagine that you have solved the problem and that the research was done, and the scene was written.

"So, how did I do this?" you ask yourself.

Suddenly, you remember that the local library - with FREE Wi-Fi! – is only ten minutes' walk from your house!

A last example, if I may, in the book context, could be from the discussion we had above about pacing yourself throughout the book.

You find yourself having written 40,000 words of a 100,000 word book. You have 10,000 words to go until you get to the scene you intend to write that will occur in the middle of the book.

You get nervous. A little scared…

"How on earth will I be able to get from where I am now, to that scene in the middle of the book?" you ask yourself.

Wrong question.

Instead, you should imagine in your mind that you HAVE already got to the middle of the book, and you then ask SC the question, "How many chapters did I have to write between where I was in Chapter 'X', and where I am now, in the middle of the book. And what action scenes or events did I have to write about in between, en route from there to here?"

It's a different question.

To which SC will give you a useful answer!

Okay. Enough. I hope you see the point I am trying to make here.

Whenever you face a problem, adopt a different view point. Imagine that you have overcome that problem, and ask yourself just how you did it.

And when you sit facing a blank page, suffering from writer's block, and not knowing what to write about in that next chapter, imagine instead that you have already written the chapter and ask SC to tell you what you wrote in it.

Then write it.

Chapter 15

Editing (Part One): Edit As You Go!

Writing can be fun!

I love it!

But…there is one part which I, personally, do not like.

And I think that few people will.

It's called editing.

Some people argue that it's the most important part of the bok.

Sorry, that should have said 'book'. (I'll have to edit and correct that part later!)

People have different ways of writing. Some writers create the first draft of their book, and then go back and edit the document only when the first draft is finished.

Others edit it on screen as they go.

Another option is to print off everything you have written each day, and then edit that the same day. Basically, you write in the morning, edit early afternoon, and then correct on screen all the mistakes you found earlier that day.

Authors/writers who can afford it - it's not cheap – pay professional editors to polish up the first draft.

Most beginners, however, probably rely on themselves to do the first few rounds of editing, and then hand the book to their friends and ask them to read it and pass judgement…and 'please, if you can, mark-up any mistakes you find on the way?'

So how do I do it?

Well, I write one or two chapters a day when I'm in the middle of writing a book. I have a day job and a family so I only get about an hour each day to write, in the evening.

I sit down and let the creative juices flow, and try to let SC tell me as clearly as possible what my fingers should be typing.

When I've hit my target for that day/evening, I print off my pages, then take a break.

Before I go to bed that evening, I find the time to sit down somewhere quiet, or take it to bed, then read what I've written that day. Whenever I find a mistake, I underline it on the page, and make a mark in the border to indicate the mistake. I find that if you don't do that, you might miss the mistakes later on when you're going through the pages.

If I find a bit that's rubbish, boring, repetitive, or doesn't make sense, I might write new text in the border area of the page with a line linking it to where it should go in the main text, or I simply make a mark and jot down a note that it needs to be rewritten.

When the first draft is complete, I clean my office, get all the pages with the corrections on them, and then spend several days or weeks going through the book, correcting all the mistakes found, and generating Version Two of the book.

Then I print off the book, read the whole book from beginning to end, mark down all the mistakes and suggested edits that I have found, and then spend the next few days correcting everything. Again.

I may then do this one more time.

What happens next is what we will discuss in Part Two of this chapter topic.

Chapter 16

Build A Pile And Watch It Grow!

The Irvine Method of writing is all about motivation.

Creating motivation, building motivation and maintaining it as you slowly (or rapidly!) create your book, and move from Page 1 with a word count of 'Zero' to the last page with a word count of approximately 100,000. (Or more, depending upon your strategy and how carried away you get!)

So, I think that I need to share with you another tip for building motivation, which I personally find incredibly satisfying.

In fact, I love it.

Before I start my book, I clean my office. I make lots of fresh, empty space. It's part of the ceremony of preparing my mind for the creation of something new. I start my book with a blank canvas and a blank office space!

On my floor beside my desk I have a special area.

Each day, as described in the last chapter, I print off my output from that day and then edit it.

Once I have edited the text by marking it up on the pages, I put those pages on the floor beside my desk. In my special book place.

On the first day, there are only a few pages.

Not much.

But I look at it and think, "*I've started!*"

I give myself a small pat on the back.

Then the next day, I add another chapter or two to the pile.

That's between five and ten pages.

I smile at the pile of pages.

The book is now definitely underway!

Each day after that, I repeat the same ritual.

Each day the pile grows.

When I get to about fifty pages in the pile, I pick it up and feel how heavy it is.

Actually, it's not very heavy at all, but it has substance. The pile is getting bigger.

What's more, not only can I TOUCH my book as it begins to develop and grow, but I can also PICK IT UP.

It's real!

The book which I have been thinking about for years, which I've been planning and playing with in my mind, is now growing every day!

Day by day, week by week, the pile grows bigger.

And bigger.

Soon it's over a hundred pages!

Then weeks later two hundred!

Fantastic!

Over half-way there…

Now, soon, only a third to go.

What? Amazing… I'm almost there…!

And then one day, you ceremoniously put down the last few pages on top of the pile and then bend down and pick the whole book up!

Your FIRST DRAFT!

The FIRST DRAFT of YOUR BOOK is complete.

You pick the book up.

You feel how heavy it is!

You put it on the desk in front of you.

And stare at it!

Why not get your camera out and photograph it!

Tweet it to your friends or relatives!

Put it on Facebook?

Then slowly it dawns on you, that you are now a real, REAL writer!

You have finished the first draft of your book. Possibly your *first* book!

No one can ever take that away from you.

Visualise that moment.

That can be you too.

Very soon!

We're not quite there yet…but almost.

There are just a few more things you need to do…

Chapter 17

Tying Up Loose Ends

The end of your novel is now perilously close. Oh dear…it's getting very exciting! Soon you will have achieved your dream and become a writer who can tell everyone that you have written a book!

Hopefully between you (your conscious self and your subconscious self) you will have conjured up an incredible story that will keep your readers enthralled from the first page to the last.

It is very likely, however, that during your story journey, you may have created several sub-plots to keep your readers entertained.

Your characters may have asked questions that need answers.

Action sequences may have been initiated in earlier chapters, but were they completed in later ones?

In other words, as we approach the end of the book, steaming through the last chapters, we do actually need to take stock of where we are.

Your conscious self needs to start checking what SC has created.

Has SC, or your conscious self, introduced threads into the storyline that need resolving?

Can you think of any actions that are outstanding and need to be completed or enacted?

Are there any loose threads that need tying up?

Are you on track to bring everything together in a wonderful, climactic last chapter where the readers go, "Wow!" and you do a fist-punch in the air and open a bottle of champagne?

If not, you need to scribble down some notes on what loose ends you think there are, and then you need to ask SC to plan to resolve these in the coming chapters.

Perhaps you already know what you need to do.

If not, you will need to consider how to deal with outstanding issues.

Here you have choices.

Either you can go back into the earlier chapters and edit those threads out...perhaps they are actually not necessary for the story after all?

Or you can simply address the outstanding threads very simply by introducing snippets of conversations between characters that talk to those points directly, and thus deal with them?

If the threads are more major, do they need to have their own chapters that address those points? Your characters may have to do extra things, or get involved in those plot areas again to resolve those points.

Perhaps you may suddenly realise that you had missed out something major, but now you have remembered it, everything will be much better and things will come together again more tightly?

In deciding how you are going to address these loose ends, you must protect the tension and excitement that you are hopefully building within your plotline as you near the end of the book.

What you DON'T want to do, is to suddenly go off on a tangent to fix something that actually steers the reader away from the main action.

e.g. The Hero is chasing after the serial killer and is JUST about to catch him, when he sees an old friend whom he borrowed ten pounds from earlier in the book, so he stops chasing the serial killer and goes and pays his friend the money he owes.

NO!

Obviously, this is a ridiculous example, but hopefully you get the point.

The reason I am raising the 'loose end issue' just now, is because readers have incredible memories. If you don't tie up the loose ends, when they get to the last page, and read those incredible words 'The End', instead of going 'Wow!', they will shift uncomfortably in their seats and exclaim, *'That's not the end... what about....?'*

Which is the last thing you want.

On the other hand, when all the loose ends are tied off and everything comes together nicely, your readers will comment on it and be amazed.

They will then recommend your book to their friends and post positive reviews on Amazon.

Which is what we all want.

But don't worry too much. If you can't remember what they are, then when you proof-read the book during the editing stages, you can take notes, and make sure you then fix any issues you spot later on.

Also, when you hand your book to your friends, relatives or professional editors, you can ask them to spot any issues that may need fixing.

So, all I'm suggesting you do at this stage, is to be cognisant of any commitments or sub-plots you may have made or initiated during earlier parts of the book, and do your best to deal with them in your first draft as you near the end of the book.

It's easier, I think, to fix these things in the first draft than in future revisions.

So, good luck thinking about those loose ends.
Find them.
Then either cut out those threads, or tie them up!

Chapter 18

Two Magic Words: 'The End'

Writing a book is all about visualisation and imagination.

At the start of the process it's all about seeing in your mind's eye, the finished product, which *you* have written.

We talk about it as if it has already happened.

We look backwards upon problems we may encounter along the journey and question how we *got over* the problems, not what we should do to *get over* them.

We visualise the shape of the story, with a firm beginning, a defined ending, and a middle.

Then we imagine, visualise and create each chapter en route to that wonderful ending that we know we will reach.

For some people who become highly motivated, once they can so clearly see the end-product, and they know in their bones that it will be done, the actual writing of the book can almost become an annoyance. They can imagine and feel so strongly that the book *has* been written, that actually writing it is a chore. However, I caution you – even if you can see the book in your mind's eye, and you can really, strongly imagine yourself holding your finished book aloft and waving it at the world, YOU STILL NEED TO WRITE THE BOOK!

Others, on the other hand, do not see the writing process as a chore.

They are very excited.

They enjoy every step of the process, and revel in the special time they get to spend sitting at their laptops or computers or smartphones writing the story.

They love the time they get to spend sitting, writing, creating new worlds with new characters, all doing their bidding, enacting actions and scenes that spring out of their imaginations…They create new virtual worlds that they design and make real.

Through the power of words, they manage to escape their own realities, and create new worlds for others, where the readers can be excited, be happy, and feel emotions they often can't in their own lives.

Writers give of themselves, and just hope, nervously, that what they have to give will be warmly received by those who read their work.

Not everyone gets to do this.
If you do, you are special.
There are BILLIONS of people on the planet.
Few ever get the time to write a book.
Few know how.
But you do.

There is a book inside you just bursting to get out, and hopefully having read *this* book, you now feel more confident about the process of how you can let this happen and now write *yours*.

The last chapter and the last two words of the book, any book, are special.

It's where you get to spring a last surprise on the reader and make them do the "wow!" thing.

It's also when and where you get to transform from one type of human being to another.

From '*One day, I'm going to write a book!*' and everyone sighs, smiles and humours you, to '*I'm a writer. I've written a book!*' and everyone smiles, lifts their eyebrows and asks, '*What's it about? Can I read it?*'

Writers are special people.

So, as you head towards the last chapter and 'The End', as the end of the first book looms into sight, you *should* and *will* start to feel a new and fresh bout of motivation.

You will find yourself finding extra time to sit down at your computer. You'll find more excuses to ignore your family and the rest of the world and lock yourself away with …yourself …just you and SC. The perfect team!

While still paying attention to the last chapter about tying up loose ends - the excitement builds and builds.

However, don't forget what I just said above.

In your rush to finish the book, don't neglect the opportunity that exists for you and SC to come up with a *brilliant* ending.

Don't just go for the ending that everyone expects you to write.

Try to come up with something better.

In fact, if you can predict how people think it will end, then take note of that, and then do something completely different.

If SC and yourself have been 'canny' – a brilliant Scottish word meaning clever and crafty – then you will have led your readers down the garden path to expect one ending, only to find that you give them another.

Most readers will love that.

The unexpected!

And when they write their reviews, they will tell the world!

"*I never saw it coming!*"

As I have gained more experience in writing, one of the things I now try to avoid is helping my readers guess the correct ending in advance.

The trick, I believe, and which I would like you to consider also, is to get your readers engaged by letting them think they are clever by telegraphing an ending, which then encourages them to read on just to see if they were correct. When they find out they were wrong, they initially feel a little disappointment but they then smile and laugh. If you're lucky, at that point there follows an outpouring of respect for you.

Which then comes out in the reviews.

"*The writer tricked me! I was sure I knew the ending, but I was wrong! I LOVE THIS WRITER!*"

The words, 'The End', are two words that can also be hugely motivational, not just as you approach them in the final stages of your book, but at any point of writing the book when you find it hard going.

When this happens, you can either go back to the chapter on 'motivating yourself to write' and do the mental exercises again, or you can perform a short-cut, by closing your eyes and imagining yourself typing those two magic words 'The End.'

Imagine yourself typing the words.

Imagine the feeling of satisfaction you will feel.

Picture that scene in your mind.

Ask SC to help you get there.

See it in your mind's eye, and it will happen!

Let me share one more secret with you.
Something very exciting indeed.

You might not realise it, or even be thinking about it yet, but those two words can be hugely misleading.

The End?

Not at all.

For many of you, it will only be *The Beginning.*

Having written one book, you will find another one on the way.

Having woken up your inner SC, unless you tell him/her to shut up, you will find new ideas pouring into your head.
SC will soon be nagging you once more sit down at your writer's desk, and start Book Number Two.

The wonderful thing is, most of you will do exactly just that.

Once a writer, ALWAYS a writer!

CONGRATULATIONS!

YOU ARE A WRITER!

Chapter 19

Editing (Part Two):

Editing What You've Written Using Enemies, Friends And

An Electronic Partner

You've written your first draft!
Amazing.
Incredible!
Brilliant!

Do not underestimate this achievement.

Getting here has been no mean feat.

That's all the good news.

Now here comes the bad news.

You're only half-done.

Up until this point you have been heavily dependent upon SC doing most of your work for you. SC has done an outstanding job of helping you create the plot, conjure up the characters and get you through the beginning, middle and to the end. Now, however it is up to you to take over. At some point you probably suspected that your conscious self would have to pull its own weight somewhere.
From now on, the next part depends upon you.
It's called editing.
The best analogy I can give you for this, is one where I compare what you now have to do with the job of a sculptor.
This is the part where you take a block of stone, look at and sense the intrinsic beauty hidden with the block of granite before you, and then chisel out of it a beautiful statue.
Editing is a bit like that.

Hidden within your first draft is almost definitely a thing of beauty. A wonderful story just hiding behind all the spelling mistakes, grammar mistakes, repetitions of overused words, repetitions of overused words, repetitions of overused words that readers really find very annoying, overuse of a good name – there are three people all called James! - and plot errors which you may not have spotted before. ('*I thought SC killed off Peter on Page 10, but in the third last chapter he walked back into a new scene completely unharmed!*')

Also, why do all my characters have names that begin with letters that are near the start of the alphabet? – there's an Alice, an Anne, an Amelia, an Alexander and an Alec, but nobody beginning with M,N,O,P, Q,R,S,T,U etc...Don't be Name-lazy!

Plus, there could be some chapters which are just rubbish. The writing is terrible, or the chapters lack punch and are very boring. Obviously, SC was not on the ball that day, or, just perhaps, maybe you were at a party the night before and you had a hangover the day you wrote those chapters? Or England lost the World Cup Rugby series and you, perhaps being English... were...just ...fed up?

Maybe, also, a scene is set wrong, the descriptions are not great, and the plot simply doesn't work. You tried your best, but some chapters just need to be better. Perhaps SC is not to blame...you may have to entertain the thought that actually, it's your fault. SC tried, but on some days, you just didn't deliver.

Don't worry! During the Editing Phase you have a chance to put all that right. You have a second chance to demonstrate to SC that you can pull your weight in the relationship and that you will turn it all around.

From the fire, a phoenix will still yet arise.

Actually, that last part was probably a little dramatic on my behalf. The chances are that your first draft is actually quite good, and not as awful as I just hinted at. I just wanted to emphasise the point.

I can, however, guarantee that there will be 'a million' mistakes in the book that need fixing. (By a million I mean *a lot*. Not literally a million. Or at least, I would hope not!)

It's important that at this point we should force ourselves to accept that we are just about to enter a new stage of the book writing process.

Instead of *praising yourself* for accomplishing what you obviously have, (can you remember how tall and heavy that pile of pages actually was? Great job!) I now want you to start being *highly critical* of your achievement, to pull it apart, and then once you've been cruel, cynical and ruthless about every word you've written, then and only then, to put it all back together again.

At that point we will have created what we will lovingly call 'The Second Draft'.

So how do you do this? How is it achieved?

Quite simply, you read your own book from cover to cover, and every time you spot something wrong, you take a big red pen to your text and either score words out, make notes to add some in, or add a comment on the side of the page about what you may need to do to make something right.

When you're reading, trying to spot all the obvious mistakes mentioned above, I also want you to look out for bits in the book where you begin to either lose interest in what you yourself have written, or where you struggle to make sense of the flow of a sentence.

Are there sentences which are toooooooo looooonnnnnng?

Or too short?

Do all the sentences flow smoothly, keeping up the pace, or are there some sentences or paragraphs which you have to read several times to understand clearly what is being said?

Are there any parts, or paragraphs which read beautifully but actually add nothing to the story and detract from the pace of the plot?

When you have marked up everything you can find wrong with your book - and remembering at all times that the more mistakes you can find, the better it will be! - you then start the painful and laborious process of sitting down and going through the whole manuscript page by page and editing the word document on your computer.

Now that's a long sentence. It could perhaps do with some editing!

When this is done, guess what?

Cough…how about, printing it all off and reading the whole manuscript again?

Ah…okay, before you do, let me tell you something important.

Writers can become blind to their own writing. By that I mean, there are certain mistakes which you never spot when rereading the same text repeatedly. Even if you know that a paragraph or sentence may contain a mistake, you may still find it difficult to find!

It's almost as if, and I actually think this may be possible, that your subconscious and conscious self have memorised all the words on each page and when you read them, you read what you *think* is there, and not what is *actually* there.

So, how do you get around this, I hear you ask?

I will suggest three ways.

Firstly, you print off the text in a different size, and a different font from normal.

Secondly, you mix up the pages and read them in a non-sensical order so that you are not reading the story, and hence skimming over the words, but are just reading *the words* because the story does not flow from one random page to another.

Thirdly, after you have revised and produced your third draft, you turn to an automatic software editing package.

My suggestion is '*ProWritingAid*', although I know there are others out there. This is an amazing piece of software that scans any text you highlight and will produce a long list of many different types of spelling mistakes, grammar mistakes, repetitive words, clichés, etc. It highlights them in different colours and you can then make your way through the sections of text you have fed into the program, and then focus on each highlighted word or expression in turn.

By the time you have fed the whole manuscript through the software programme, and have addressed whatever it throws up at you, you will have removed many of the remaining mistakes.

I suggest you run the manuscript through the software twice, and use as much of the available functionality as possible to help prune, tune and polish your novel.

When this is done, I have a few more suggestions for you.

Although the software packages you can buy now are truly excellent, they still do not pick up all the mistakes. A classic example may be a stray word. A stray word may be spelt correctly, and may not seem to break any programmable laws of grammar, but when you read it with your human eye, you immediately see that the word is out of context, or is just obviously wrong. Sometimes this can come about when the writing package you are using auto-corrects a word you have spelt wrongly, but automatically replaces it with the wrong word.

For example, you may have been wanting to write, "*The man ate his favourite food*", but you misspelt the word food, and the writing programme automatically corrects it to '*foot*'.

In this case, the spelling and grammar programme you may be using to correct your book may find nothing wrong with the word '*foot*', but clearly, it would be rather strange if we were to write about a man eating his favourite foot.

To help weed out all the remaining spelling mistakes or misplaced words, and to find any remaining plot inconsistencies or unfinished story lines that need to be tied up, you need the help of other human beings.

I suggest you find someone who loves to read, but who does not know you very well. You ask politely if they would be interested in reading your work, but with a critical eye.

Most people would love to do this.

For many this becomes a personal challenge.

Not everyone can write a book, but it seems that many people in this world possess the inborn ability to put other people down and be critical.

So, if you ask someone to find and highlight your mistakes, most people jump at the chance.

It's almost as if, the more mistakes they can find, the more superior they are to you.

Little do they know, that this is exactly what you want!

Having exhausted your own conscious self in the hunt for mistakes, you now actively seek to engage the conscious self of others, and get them to do work for you.

The more mistakes they find the better.

With luck they will demonstrate how wonderfully superior they are to you, by finding every remaining mistake in your book!

Of course, there are others who you will meet who will do this because they are actually very decent, lovely people who just want to help.

I am blessed by knowing some of these, who help me with each of my new books, but from an editing perspective, I would welcome both.

In the hunt for edits, I don't care who finds them, I am quite mercenary.

I just want to find them. Root them out. Edit them. And get rid of them!

In the editing process, there is one entire class of human being that should never be involved in the editing process or asked to give any realistic critical assessments of your books.

They are called 'Friends and Relatives'.

Most of these types of human simply do not want to upset you or fall out with you. They could not be critical of your work if they tried.

When you hand your manuscript over to them and ask them to find mistakes and then share an honest opinion with you of what they think about it, the manuscript comes back almost blank.

"Did you like it?" you will inevitably ask, since they are being quite silent and just smiling.

In reply, they smile back.

"I loved it." They reply. "It was wonderful."

"Can you suggest any ways to improve it?" you may enquire further.

"No. It was almost perfect," your mother, or your brother or sister, or your favourite aunt will reply.

You must forgive them.

They think they are being critical. But,…they are just so proud of you, and you were such a cute two year old, that how could they ever say anything negative about you?

So, I think you get the picture.

When it comes to editing, ignore anything your friends and relatives say! They can't really help you.

Now comes the Public Health and Procrastination warning. Pay attention!

Extended editing can seriously damage the health of your novel.

By that I mean some people get so scared about ever releasing an imperfect novel to the world, that they edit a book to death.

Once the writer has got himself/herself into an introspective, error-hating, mistake-hunting mindset, rather than risk the opinion of a reader who could possibly read the book and criticise it if it were ever published, they become scared of actually finishing the book and publishing it.

I've known people to spend years editing a book, determined to make it 'perfect'.

In the Irvine Method, we make sure this does not happen.

The purpose of the Irvine Method is to produce a book that tells a story so that others can read it.

The trick is to identify when a book is *almost* perfect, not when it is 100% perfect.

It's better to get the book out there, and published, so others can read it, than spend too long editing, delaying and procrastinating.

So, how do you know when it's ready?

For me, it's when I hand the book over to a person who doesn't really know me, and when they hand the book back a week or a few days later, and they have nothing really negative to say.

"I found two mistakes?" they may say. "I'll show them to you. Were they the ones you were looking for?"

"Yes," you reply. "They're the ones I wanted to find."

Two mistakes? Or eight?

That's hardly any!

I think you're now at the point of diminishing returns.

After you've corrected these few mistakes, instead of spending the next few weeks chasing down any new ones, I think it's time to take off the editing hat, and put on the publishing hat.

But, before we get to that chapter, I think you need to read the next chapter very seriously, and complete all the instructions it gives you.

Chapter 20

YOU ARE A WINNER

CONGRATULATIONS!!!

Having now completed the editing stage and got to your second or third draft I
want you to take stock of what you will have achieved by the time you get to this point.

Some of you will be reading this chapter now for a second time: you read it once before you started your book, and now again, having just completed your latest draft.

The bottom line is, that by the time you get to here you will have achieved something amazing!

You will be a writer.

You will have written a book!

Think about this. It's an incredible achievement. Writing a book is only a dream for most people.

But you may have written one by the time you read this chapter. And that's amazing!

If you have not yet written your book, I want you to imagine the feeling of what it will be like when you come back to this chapter in later months and read these words with a full novel now behind you!

Imagine how that will feel.

So, whether you have done it already - or you will have done it when you read these words again and for now you still just need to imagine what it feels like - pat yourself on your back!

When I wrote these words, there were 7.8 billion people in the world.

Only a tiny, miniscule fraction of that population will have ever written a book.

That makes you very, very special.

Let's try to put that into perspective.

You may be the only person in your school to have grown up and published a book!

You may be the first person in your family to have written a book!

You may be the first person in your village, town or even city to have published a book, depending upon where you live!

Out of all the people you have ever met in your life, you may be the only author.

Can you see how special that makes you?

So, please, close your eyes for a moment, mentally pat yourself on your back, and thank SC for all his/her help.

If you have a bottle of champagne in the house, I think you are entitled to, and really should, open it and share a drink with your loved ones.

You are amazing!

And that's official!

Chapter 21

Time To Decide: Publish or Self-Publish?

Your novel is finished.

It's sitting there in a neat pile on the table in front of you.

So, what do you do with it now?

The big question you have to answer is whether or not you are going to go down the self-publishing route (Independent/'Indie'), or the traditional (Trad) publishing route.

Until about 2011, when Amazon opened up its doors for authors to Self-Publish through their Kindle Direct Publishing service, authors didn't really have much choice. If they wanted to see their book in print, they had to approach literary agents and publishing houses in order to get a publishing contract. Alternatively, they could PAY someone to publish their book and put in it print. The latter practice earned the nickname 'Vanity Publishing' because it was targeted at people who wanted to see their books printed, regardless of how good they were.

I would not recommend anyone to go down the Vanity Publishing route. If you are not careful, you could also find yourself falling victim to a scam.

Thanks to Amazon this is also no longer necessary.

As well as offering writers the opportunity to become proper authors by publishing their books in electronic format which can be read on their Kindle electronic readers, it now also offers the possibility of Digital Publishing. This enables writers to upload their text into special software on Amazon which then allows the writer to arrange and edit the text and layout on the pages of a virtual book. Once you have also uploaded a cover design and blurb for the back page, you can then quite literally order as many copies of a paperback version of the book as you wish. Even if you want to order just one copy, you can. It will arrive several days or possibly weeks later depending how you order it and where you live. When it arrives, you will have your very own copy of your very own book!

And, the good news continues: today you can even work with different companies to produce Audio Versions of your books, where voice actors will read your book aloud and record it so that readers – or listeners – can download the book and enjoy it simply by listening to it.

Amazon is not the only company offering this capability, but it is by far the most popular amongst readers and authors alike.

So, now you have your own book, which path should you decide to go down? Trad Pub or Indie Pub?

This is a difficult question to answer, and to be honest, even I don't know the answer to this. However, the following paragraph may put the answer into perspective for you.

I've been writing books since 1995. I've now written about twenty books.

Each and every one of them has been rejected by publishers throughout the UK.

I have every right to feel incredibly rejected and downhearted.

Yet, I do not.

Why?

Because thanks to the Indie Publishing revolution I have had the opportunity to find an audience for my work.

So far, I've had very close to two million books downloaded from Amazon, which is my main funnel for distributing my books via their KDP Service.

That's TWO MILLION copies of my books.

ALL OVER THE WORLD!

There are people who've read my books in countries across the globe that I will never visit.

It's worthwhile considering that if I had been successful in the Trad Pub route, my books would probably only have been published in certain countries, so my distribution would never have reached those countries across the globe where some people now actually know my name!

However, so far, I have never walked into a bookshop and seen my books on their shelves.

If you don't have a Kindle, the chances are you will not have heard of me, and even if you do have a Kindle, the chances are that you still will not have heard of me. Sadly, I continue to be a small fish in a very big pond.

I still dream of the winning a big book deal with a mainstream publishing house. I still want my books to be found in the large bookshops, sitting on those shelves and tables just beside the entrance, inviting readers to pick them up, skim through their pages, and then BUY THEM!!!! (*Please.*)

Yet, even though my books have amassed large numbers of five-star reviews on Amazon - at one time I had the highest rated 'thriller' available on Amazon Prime that month! - I am continually still rejected by mainstream publishers.

I don't know why.

Yet, I still dream the dream.

One day, I am determined, I *will* be given a deal.

Increasingly though, thanks to the Indie Revolution in publishing, at the end of the day, each author seriously has to ask themselves why they still want to be published by a mainstream publisher?

When comparing each of the possible routes, Indie versus Trad, the questions most authors ask themselves include:

1. How many books will I sell?
2. How much money will I earn?
3. How long will I have to wait before my book is published?
4. Who owns the rights to my book after publication?
5. Who will market my book?
6. Will I be able to give up my day job to write full-time?

Unfortunately, except to say that most Indie authors retain the rights to their own books, I can't provide detailed answers to most of these questions, especially the first two. All I can report is that if you type in a question into your internet browser, such as: 'How much money do Authors earn?' the answer will surprise you.

It's not very much.

In the UK it's commonly reported that authors earn less than the average UK wage, which means that it's not really possible for most authors to give up their day job. In other countries it's the same.

Yet, we all know that a small percentage of traditionally published authors make vast fortunes. They become household names. Famous, wealthy and loved by many adoring fans. They travel the world speaking at book fairs, and regularly give TV interviews.

Indie Authors on the other hand are largely unknown.

Almost no one knows who I am, but according to the figures, my books sales are higher than many traditionally published authors.

Yet, no one knows who I am.

I think that for me, were I offered a contract, I'd probably take it so that I could see my books in the bookshops. I'm still vain that way. It's part of my personal dream.

In the meantime, I continue to pursue my dream, but by doing everything myself.

I do my own editing, formatting, publishing on Amazon, and my own marketing, of which I admit I do very little indeed.

The answer to the third question above really depends upon how impatient you are, and what your long-term book publishing aims are.

It's worth considering that if you get a Trad-book contract, it may be two to three years before your book ends up in print and in circulation; this compares with six to twelve months if you sign up with a Digital Publisher who focusses on the ebook market.

Yet, if you decide to publish it yourself, on Amazon KP or any of the other routes available (i.e. directly with Apple or Kobo or Barnes & Noble or Google Play, or via distributors such as Smashwords, Draft2Digital, IngramSpark or PublishDrive etc.) once you have a number of key assets available at your fingertips, you can publish your book to the world in a matter of minutes, not days, weeks, months or years!

Assets that you may need to gather together to help you self-publish an ebook for example, may include:

- A book cover designed for use on an ebook platform or the front cover of a printed book.
- A catchy blurb to describe your book
- Keywords which you have chosen to help position your book within the relevant categories on your ebook retailer

- A digital file containing your book in a format acceptable to the ebook retailer
- A decision on the genres/categories where your book will appear, i.e. Romance, Crime, Science Fiction
- An understanding of how the ebook platform will sell your book and which royalty scheme you will be entitled to, which may guide you as to the price you wish to sell your book for
- An ISBN number (not all ebook platforms will require this: some platforms will offer to provide you one for free, or will offer an alternative e.g. Amazon will allocate you an ASIN which is their equivalent).

In a previous chapter we have talked about the ebook cover. If you decide to Self-Publish, a high-quality ebook cover is absolutely necessary.

Also, a catchy blurb that immediately hooks a reader and motivates them to download your ebook from an ebook product page is also something you need to spend time on.

A small piece of good news for you, is that directions to where you can find guidance on these topics can be found in the Bonus Chapter of this book!

If you know any authors, you may wish to have a discussion with them about the pros and cons of either Trad or Indie Publishing.

You can also go online and simply type in '*Indie Publishing versus Traditional Publishing*' and read whatever comes back: you'll be swamped for choice.

Okay, that's probably enough for now on this topic. I just wanted to highlight that when you get to this stage, you will be faced with this choice. Many people have already written a lot on this topic, and it's not the focus of this book, which is to motivate you in your book writing journey so that you write a book and then ultimately *do* end up with this choice.

It's actually a privileged choice to be presented with. Few people are. Enjoy it when it comes!

Chapter 22

Doing Research For Your Books

I never wrote the first book I wanted to write.

I started it.

Then I spent weeks locked in a library in Scotland trying to dig up as much historical detail as I possibly could about my intended topic.

I wanted to write a historical thriller.

I still hope to write it one day.

A number of weeks into my project, I realised that I was drowning in the research I needed to do. I also realised that when I began to weigh up how much research I was going to have to do on an almost ongoing basis, versus my motivation to write the book and the practicality of writing it, that I should probably abandon the project and write something very different that didn't need so much research.

That was in 1992.

Now it's 2019.

As far as research is concerned, everything has changed.

Now I do a lot of research. Yet, instead of spending hours going back and forward to the library, climbing ladders and lifting heavy tomes of knowledge off the top shelves, before blowing off the dust and the cobwebs, these days I simply type in a question into my browser of choice, and within seconds, voilà, everything I've ever needed to know about something is listed there, before my eyes, and only one click away.

It's got to the point that you can start a chapter knowing that half-way through you will need to research everything there is to know about a topic, no matter how obscure, and when you come to the point you need it, you ask the internet to tell you what you need, and it's provided. Another term I could coin for the internet is 'knowledge-on-demand'!

This doesn't mean that I don't do my research. I just wanted to emphasise how simple it is now. The Internet has made all our writers' lives so much simpler.

A particularly special place to learn knowledge is YouTube.

If you've ever wondered how to do 'X', 'Y' or 'Z', it's practically guaranteed that you can go to YouTube and find an expert somewhere who has made a video on your particular topic of choice.

As a writer, don't underestimate the resources which you now have, quite literally, at your fingertips.

Only one click away.

It's a resource you should and must use.

So, now don't be worried about doing research. You should even prepare yourself for the possibility that you might enjoy it!

When I wrote this chapter and looked at YouTube, I even managed to find this:

https://www.youtube.com/watch?v=AtrhWDD9-pU

(It's a little old, and I'd even forgotten I'd made it!)

Chapter 23

How Many Pages Should I Write Each Day?

It depends how motivated you are to write, and how much you are enjoying your time spent alone writing your novel and moving closer to your dream of having written a book. It also depends on whether or not you have a job, or a family to bring up.

I do not want to ever hear that one of you has been sitting at your computer for days on end, and has forgotten to feed your family, who are now starving to death and considering eating each other! If it's your responsibility to feed and look after them, do that first. Before you write!

Personally, I try to write one or two chapters a day. That equates to between two thousand or four thousand words a day. Beyond that I need time out to go for my walk, or to swim, and to think about the chapters ahead and how I will write them.

As my children grow up, I am spending less and less time actually writing, and more time learning the role of a taxi-driver.

One day, we will have driver-less cars, and I will be allowed to return to my desk and finish my books. Until then, I personally am limited on the number of words I can churn out each day.

I've heard that other authors are able to sit and write all day long. They are highly motivated, love to write, and their creativity never seems to dry up.

I do not however, advocate just sitting at your computer and writing for writing's sake. If you run out of meaningful things to say, or you are waiting for SC to give you the next part of the story, then get up, leave your office, and go and do something else.

Only come back and sit down when you can feel the words filling up the end of your fingers and getting ready to burst out.

The last word on this, is that books don't write themselves. So, establishing some form of discipline whereby you do sit down at your computer every day and try to write, is a good practice to engage in.

You will find that SC is a highly tameable creature. If he/she knows you will be sitting down to write between, for example, 8 and

10 p.m. every night, then that's when you will feel the inspiration begin to well up from within.

It will become the tap you turn on when you sit down to write, and which you turn off when you've reached your daily target, or when your fingers begin to hurt.

On that last point, make sure you have a comfortable chair, your desk is the right height, and your computer screen is level with your head. Ensuring you have the right posture when writing is essential, especially if you think this is an activity you may continue to engage in when your first book is done.

In this book I have tried to help make sure that 'Writer's Block' never becomes a problem for you, however, if you develop a sore neck, or tendonitis in your fingers or arms because of excessive writing whilst sitting with a bad posture, I'm sorry, but I can't help you with that!

May I suggest you google "Posture and Seating for Writing?" You might even find a video on it on YouTube!

If you want to become a writer with a long-term career, please, look after yourself!

Before we round off this chapter, may I give you a very useful tip that could save you hours or potentially even years of work?

I just wanted to emphasise that when you write a book, which could take days, months, or even years of effort, it is extremely wise to 'save' your work continuously as you write. After every few pages, SAVE YOUR DOCUMENT!

Not only in one place, but in several!

When I write, I routinely create two documents: 'Main Document', and a backup document 'Main Document Back-up'.

I then also REGULARLY save my work to an external hard-drive or a flash stick.

Nowadays, you also have the option to save your work to or in 'the cloud', in some way. To investigate these options, why not type in *'How do I save to cloud for free?'* into your browser, then explore the options that come up?

Lastly, I also back up my work onto an external flash-stick or hard-drive and bury it in a box in my garden. Why? Because if my house is burnt down or broken into, and all my storage media are destroyed or stolen, then I can dig up my own treasure from the garden and not worry about losing anything.

You may think that I am being paranoid.

No, I am not.

One day my computer just stopped working. I couldn't reboot that computer. I lost everything.

Last month, Microsoft decided to update my wife's computer with a software patch that essentially erased access to every file stored on that computer. She lost everything, or so she had thought…Cleverly, I had backed everything up to an external drive the month before, so she effectively lost very little.

What really worries me however, is a cyber ransomware attack, where somehow you accidentally download some malware onto your computer, and a hacker takes over your computer files and encrypts them so you can't read them. They then send you an email demanding payment in 'bitcoins' to their private account, threatening never to give you access to your computer files again unless you pay up!

All the above bad scenarios can be avoided if you have made backups.

Lastly, I would suggest you go that extra mile and regularly send or give a copy of your data to your sister/brother or a friend who lives hundreds of miles from you.

Why?

Because if your house floods, and the garden is under water, and someone breaks into your house and steals your external hard-drive or your computer, all you have to do is buy a new computer and get the files back from your friend/relative, who will not have been affected by your local natural disaster.

If you still think I'm being paranoid, consider this: imagine you have been writing for twenty years. Everything you have written is on your computer and/or media hidden in your house. One day your house blows up in a gas explosion and you lose everything. If you have backed everything up, then you can easily get everything back.

Twenty years of writing is a lot of work. Take precautions. Write safely. Be careful!

By the way, I would suggest you also do this for all your photographs! Personally, I think my digital photographs of my family, relatives and friends are my most treasured possessions, with my books firmly in second place.

It's just advice. Take it or leave it. But please don't regret not taking it!

Chapter 24

Celebrate! The End Is Nigh!

The purpose of this book has been to provide a practical, inspirational guide on how to approach writing a new book. The book focuses on generating internal motivation and using the power of your Subconscious Creative Self to achieve your dream of writing a novel.

Without stepping on the toes of many other authors who may have written extensively on how you should or shouldn't write a book or which provide guidance or advice on how to develop characters and storylines, I hope that I have managed to take you through the basics of how to approach the task.

I don't claim to be a good writer, but I have written quite a few books, and I know how that aspect of things is done, and this book is about the process and not the result.

Luckily, if you read the reviews associated with my books on Amazon, it would seem that many readers, particularly those in the UK, seem to enjoy my work and my writing style.

Others don't, and that's okay: when I go to a bookshop, there are thousands of books on the shelves, and most of them I would never consider reading. I have specific interests and my own list of favourite authors.

I am fortunate however, in that I have had quite a lot of success as an author, and I believe a lot of that does in fact come down to the process I've outlined in this book.

Although I've been writing for many years now, I hope that I am still only at the beginning of my journey.

I can almost guarantee that some of you who are reading this book today will go on to become very successful writers. Some of you will earn A LOT of money. Others will receive tremendous praise and respect for your work. And some of you will come to be loved by millions! That won't happen to everyone. But that's not what's important here. What *is* important is that if you follow the Irvine Method outlined in these chapters, then most of you will come to fulfil the dream you have dreamt of all your lives.

You will become a writer. An author.

You will be able to put a copy of your very own book upon your own bookshelf for all your friends and relatives to see.

And for you to look at yourself with pride.

And who knows, one day, in a hundred, or perhaps even a thousand years' time, someone will pick up a copy of your book in an 'interstellar rocket-boot sale' [What were cars?] or borrow your book from a library, or buy it from an antique shop, and they will read it!

Through your book, you will live on!

In closing, first may I congratulate you for getting to this part of this book. You've read all about how to go and make your dream come true, and to write that book which is inside of you and just bursting to get out. Now you know what to do! So…

GO WRITE YOUR BOOK!

NOW!

[Cue the drum roll, here comes those two incredible words…]

The End!

P.S.

For all of you who decide to go down the Self-Publishing route, one of the most important things you can do, is to build your very own contact list of readers whom you can, in future, email and inform about your *next* book when it is published.

(I think you will love the next bit...)

So, for anyone who wants to find out HOW to build an email list, or who would also like to learn about other resources that you could highly benefit from when writing your book and when its finished (How to get an agent? How to publish it? How to market it? Sell it? Create Front Covers? Build an email list etc.), then...

Please Subscribe to my email list and I will immediately send you a Bonus Chapter to this book, which will guide you to additional, vital and very useful publishing resources that I recommend you consider! The Bonus Chapter will include information on where to find:

- Tools to help authors write books and then advertise them
- Tools to help authors grow their own email contact list
- Information on the 'Self Publishing Formula' Writing Community and Resources
- Useful Books on Writing

TO GET THE BONUS CHAPTER TYPE IN THE FOLLOWING STRING INTO YOUR FAVOURITE INTERNET BROWSER AND THEN FOLLOW THE INSTRUCTIONS!

http://eepurl.com/gJxT5X

(See what I did there? Not only am I teaching you a new, important trick, but I am also practicing what I preach!)

P.P.S.

If you sign up to my email list, I promise not to hassle you with lots of spam emails. I will only contact you with news of new books which I have written, or when I add additional information to this book in future which I feel you could benefit from or be interested in. You will be able to unsubscribe at any time if I annoy you or bore you to tears.

OTHER BOOKS BY ME THAT I THINK YOU SHOULD BUY!

(See what I'm doing there too? I'm teaching you how to sell and promote your own work! But seriously, you may want to consider getting **Haunted From Within** or **The Messiah Conspiracy** which I have referenced in this book. Fortunately for you, you will never be able to buy that Top-Drawer Novel that I told you about earlier!)

If you have any comments, please feel free to contact me at:-

iancpirvine@hotmail.co.uk

All of my books are written as a series, and are available as Omnibus Editions containing two books, or in two parts as Book One or Book Two.

Information on the Omnibus editions is given below, but almost all of my Book One editions are available for Free and can be found on Amazon or at

http://www.free-ebook.co.uk

"Have you heard about my 'Try-before-you-buy?' scheme? If you like the idea of reading Free Ebooks and only paying for the whole book if you like it, please visit my webpage of Free Ebooks at..."

http://www.free-ebook.co.uk.

My website is:

www.iancpirvine.com

For information on the other books I've written, just in case you might be interested (hint, hint!), please see the next page.

But before I go, please may I wish you ***good luck with your writing***!
When your book is published, please write to me and tell me – I would love to see it!

Lastly, if you have enjoyed this book and you have found it useful, please leave a review on Amazon, tell your friends about the book and feel welcome to write to me. I would love to hear from you!

HAPPY WRITING!

Please look out for others books by IAN C.P. IRVINE on Amazon and see below:-

I Spy, I Saw Her Die
Say You're Sorry
The Assassin's Gift
Haunted From Within
Haunted From Without
The Orlando File
The Sleeping Truth
Time Ship
London 2012: What If ?
The Messiah Conspiracy
Alexis Meets Wiziwam the Wizard

To keep up to date with other news, events and ebook releases, please visit the website at: www.iancpirvine.com

Printed in Poland
by Amazon Fulfillment
Poland Sp. z o.o., Wrocław

59637067R00056